Critical Social Studies

Editors: JOCK YOUNG and PAUL WALTON

The contemporary world projects a perplexing picture of political, social and economic upheaval. In these challenging times the conventional wisdoms of orthodox social thought whether it be sociology, economics or cultural studies become inadequate. This series focuses on this intellectual crisis, selecting authors whose work seeks to transcend the limitations of conventional discourse. Its tone is scholarly rather than polemical, in the belief that significant theoretical work is needed to clear the way for a genuine transformation of the existing social order.

Because of this, the series will relate closely to recent developments in social thought, particularly to critical theory – the emerging European tradition. In terms of specific topics, key pivotal areas of debate will be selected – for example, mass culture, inflation, problems of sexuality and the family, the nature of the capitalist state, natural science and ideology. The scope of analysis will be broad: the series will attempt to break the existing arbitrary divisions between the social studies disciplines. Its aim is to provide a platform for critical social thought (at a level quite accessible to students) to enter into the major theoretical controversies of the day.

Critical Social Studies

PUBLISHED

FORTHCOMING

Theories
of
Underdevelopment

Ian Roxborough

M

First edition 1979
Reprinted 1981 (twice)

Published by
THE MACMILLAN PRESS LTD
London and Basingstoke
Companies and
representatives
throughout the world

Printed in Hong Kong

British Library Cataloguing in Publication Data

Roxborough, Ian
    Theories of underdevelopment. – (Critical social
    studies).
    1. Underdeveloped areas – Economic conditions
    2. Economic development
    I. Title II. Series
    330.9 172′4   HC59.7

    ISBN 0–333–21189–8
    ISBN 0–333–21190–1 Pbk

Contents

Contents

Acknowledgements

The most gratifying, but perhaps the most humbling, part of writing a book is to sit down at the end of the process and acknowledge the many debts incurred by the author. First, thanks are due to Adriane Thompson, Hazel Lewis and, particularly, Judith White, for their invaluable assistance in typing the manuscript.

Over the last few years I have benefited from the comments of a number of friends and colleagues, though not always in the ways they might have wished. While formally exonerating them from responsibility for the shortcomings of this book, I would like to thank Angus Stewart, Nicos Mouzelis, Chris Rhodes, Ian Buchanan, Ronaldo Ramirez, Richie Kronish, Ken Mericle, Tom Bossert, Cris Kay and Joe Foweraker.

I have had the good fortune to study with Nigel Harris and Maurice Zeitlin. Although neither had a hand in the preparation of this book, such merits as it may have are, to a greater extent than they perhaps realise, a result of their influence.

Preface

The principal concern of this book is to explore some of the theoretical and methodological issues which arise in the study of major social change, particularly as it occurs in the contemporary Third World. However, the central premiss of the book is that a critique of theory (at least, a critique of those theories concerning social change in the Third World) cannot be adequately carried out purely at the level of theory.

The central defect of a great deal of writing on the Third World is that of overgeneralisation. It seems as if many analysts believe that one can construct a model of an underdeveloped society and its problems, as though there were some unique situation of underdevelopment, and all empirical situations were merely variations on this ideal type. There are two objections to such a procedure. The first is that the range of variation among contemporary underdeveloped societies is so great that one might reasonably baulk at trying to describe them in terms of a single model. This objection is easily met by developing several models so that no empirical society is too unlike one of these ideal types. Indeed, one might reasonably question the utility of talking about a single 'Third World', given the tremendous range of variation among the underdeveloped countries.

The second objection is of a different order. The assumption that one can take a model of an underdeveloped society and thereby analyse social processes is ahistorical. It is ahistorical in that it de-emphasises two things. On the one hand, such a model plays down the importance of the changing international context in which development takes place. As the sections on imperialism and dependency (Chapters 4 and 5) seek to illustrate, the changing international context is a key determinant of change in the Third World. Change in the social systems of the Third World is primarily exogenous, rather than endogenous. Hence, all endogenous paradigms of change are inherently suspect.

On the other hand, most models of underdeveloped societies de-emphasise the extent to which the changing economic structure produces qualitative structural changes in the class structure and gives rise to changing patterns of class alliance which have repercussions at the level of politics and the state. The forms and histories of the class structures of underdeveloped societies vary greatly and form a central part of any explanation.

The failure of much writing on the sociology of development to consider adequately the above objections results in an attempt to develop theoretical propositions at too global a level. The literature on the sociology of development is replete with propositions of the type: 'the military is a modernising force', 'the introduction of capitalism precipitates peasant revolt', 'states in the Third World are Bonapartist', 'imperialism prevents economic development', and so on.

By and large, if you take any one of these propositions, there is as much evidence for it as against it. By treating the Third World as though it were composed of a number of essentially similar units, this approach ignores the varying and differing histories of the countries of the Third World. For these propositions to have any utility, they need to be made historically specific, both in terms of the development of the world capitalist system and in terms of the way in which the articulation of the underdeveloped country with that system has generated, over time, a specific class structure and set of political institutions with their own history. To explain, for example, the relationship between military intervention and economic growth, or between peasant revolt and the commercialisation of agriculture, one must first locate the society in an historical–structural model of the development of world capitalism and then focus on the way in which the specific history of that country has affected the interrelationships between social processes. (That is, the causal relation between the variables in a theoretical model will vary from society to society in a determinate way depending on the historical process of class formation.)

This does not mean that no generalisation is possible, that we can only write a series of individual histories. Theoretical generalisation is possible, but the process is a complex one. Until it is much further advanced, it would be prudent to be modest in our attempts at generalisation.

What this book sets out to do, therefore, is to examine some common theories about development which are prevalent today and indicate the ways in which overgeneralisations need to be modified in order to produce a reasonably adequate historical and contextual explanation. The aim is not exhaustively to review all important theorists or bodies of theory. It is to take illustrative examples and use them to indicate what an adequate explanation might look like. Furthermore, the need for historical specificity has meant that I have attempted to support my arguments with concrete historical examples. Because I have worked primarily in the study of Latin American societies, most examples will be drawn from that part of the world. In general terms, I believe the analysis is applicable to most other parts of the Third World, at least as a methodological example. However, considerable substantive modifications are necessary. This is not a textbook on the problems of Third World societies because such a book is not possible at this stage of our knowledge. Nor is this book an attempt to replace one theoretical framework with another. It is not primarily an argument for the superiority of one particular set of theoretical propositions, though of course, there *is* a specific theoretical framework which organises the book. The main concern of the book is not with theory *per se*, but rather with a set of meta-theoretical or methodological issues, that is, what would an adequate theory look like?

At this stage I should say something which ought to be obvious. In this book I criticise a number of works; some of them, in my opinion, are quite poor, and others I think are excellent pieces of work. The fact of criticism itself says nothing about what I believe the merits of the book to be. It is through criticism that one learns, and it would be churlish of me not to acknowledge the great debt I owe to many authors criticised in these pages (and many others who have, perforce, been omitted).

Much of what goes under the label of social science plays an immediately ideological role. In many cases this is manifested in the nature of the language employed. It is unnecessarily obscurantist and esoteric. Its obfuscation shrouds reality in a mist of misperception and ambiguity. In some cases, recourse is had to semantic barbarisms in order to disguise a lack of substantive content or a confusion on certain points of interpretation. In this book I have tried as far as possible to dispense with sociological jargon and the private languages of particular schools of social thought.

I have not always succeeded in this. But I hope I have been sufficiently clear so that the ambiguities, errors and confusions into which I have lapsed are easily apparent to the reader. If indeed the emperor has no clothes, let this be acknowledged openly. Of course, it is my hope that this is not the case at all, and that in these pages the reader will find, if not a wardrobe of clothes for his conceptual armoury, at least the design and pattern so that he can cut his own bolt of cloth from the ever-changing reality of the world we find ourselves in.

I

The Original Transition

No society is ever static and totally unchanging; nevertheless, some changes are more important than others. From the perspective of the twentieth century, of crucial importance is a complex set of changes occurring primarily in Western Europe in the long period from the sixteenth to the nineteenth century. At some point in this period, a chain of events began which was to produce contemporary capitalism. The shape of the world was to be radically transformed. Just what these changes were, when, why and how they occurred, and the precise nature of the society to which they gave rise, are all matters of dispute. It was this attempt to understand the nature of the transition, and to come to grips with it, that gave rise to that distinctive corpus of social thought which has evolved into modern sociology. The different strands of that body of thought produced fundamentally different accounts of what had happened, and equally diverse descriptions of contemporary society. The three most important accounts are those of Marx, Weber and Durkheim. There were others, of course, both before and after, but these three thinkers have come to represent distinctive approaches to the question: for the sake of simplicity of presentation, we will concentrate on them.

All focused on the rupture, the discontinuities, between old and new. All saw modern industrial capitalism as a qualitatively new kind of society. Weber's distinctive contribution was to emphasise the way in which increasingly wider spheres of life were brought under the control of rational thought. But this process of rationalisation of the world meant that power was increasingly transferred out of the hands of traditional political leaders and into formal organisations which embodied rationality to a hitherto unknown degree – bureaucracies. Hand in hand with increasing rationalisation went increasing bureaucratic domination. This was only one aspect of the process; the incumbents of bureaucratic roles could not set goals for themselves, they could only follow orders. There had to be some source of authority over and above the bureaucratic structures of domination. With the demise of the authority of traditional leaders, this position would increasingly be usurped by charismatic leaders, upstarts from the mass, unrestrained by the ties and duties of tradition or by the rational constraints of bureaucratic norms. Their actions would be increasingly unpredictable. Yet after these outbursts of wild energy, the forces of routinisation would reassert themselves. A successor to the charismatic leader would have to be selected, the following would be transformed into an organisation, and bureaucratic routine, with its formal rationality, would once again come to the fore. Modern society would witness an oscillation, a dialectic without development, between the long periods of bureaucratic routine and irrational outbreaks of charisma.

This trend towards increasing rationalisation occurs throughout history, but it is repeatedly thwarted and turned back by traditional leaders and the great cultural institutions of religion. Throughout history, economics remains subordinate to politics, and there is no scope therefore for the thoroughgoing rationalisation of economic activity which will transform the organisation of productive activity and usher in the new age of industrial capitalism.

However, an unanticipated breakthrough occurs in the Reformation. Calvin and his followers had asserted the primacy of individual conscience and individual interpretations of the Bible in their break with the Church, with its traditional and anti-rational demand that only the Church should interpret the scriptures. Calvin claimed that men were predestined; but only some – the elect – would go to heaven. There was no way of knowing beforehand whether one belonged to the elect or not. Weber argued that this theological doctrine produced intense anxiety among the Calvinists and that, in order to reduce this anxiety and reassure themselves that they were, in fact, to be numbered among the elect, they attempted to behave as though they had indeed been called. This meant, first and foremost, a systematic ordering of their daily life, including their economic pursuits, so as to preclude any idleness or frivolity. The resulting asceticism and the intense anxiety-produced drive to show earthly signs of God's favour, led to rapid economic advance and capital accumulation. According to Weber, this, together with increases in rationalisation in other spheres of society, provided the catalyst for the development of modern industrial society, a society which, despite its individualistic origins, was to end up by providing a minimum scope for human freedom.

Throughout his writings, Weber, like the other great thinkers considered here, was concerned with the nature of the moral order which was developing. He was concerned not simply to provide a neutral account of the changes which had taken place, but also to explore the potentialities for human freedom which the new order opened up. As we have seen, his conclusions were deeply pessimistic. Weber himself was only too aware of this, and saw himself as a kind of latter-day Jeremiah, a prophet of disaster yet to come. His attitude to the changes brought about by the development of modern capitalism was fundamentally ambivalent, and tinged with nostalgia for the past.

These themes are even more pronounced in the work of his French contemporary, Emile Durkheim. For Durkheim, the central fact of the transition from traditional to modern society was the dissolution of the old ties of mechanical solidarity which bound people to each other in the tightly knit communities of pre-industrial society. The interpersonal bonds had depended on spatial contiguity and personal acquaintance, and had broken down with the changes attendant on the emergence of modern society, particularly urbanisation. These changes had led to a progressive depersonalisation of society and man could no longer turn to authoritative institutions such as the Church for spiritual guidance. The old sources of moral direction were in decay, and nothing had as yet replaced them. The soulless individualism of modern society could not cope with this problem of widespread anomie. Durkheim's prescription was the creation of new institutions to replace the old sources of moral authority with a new organic solidarity. He was one of the early corporatist theorists, and looked forward to a reintegration of human communities around the axis of corporatist guilds formed at the workplace. Anomie would give way to a new authoritative moral order. This solution was repugnant to Weber's individualistic protestantism and the Kantian emphasis on individual morality, but it did provide the basis for a major conservative critique of modern society.

Marx also was concerned with the absence of a true community among men in industrial society. He saw this state of alienation as stemming from the division of society into hostile and antagonistic classes. With the dispossession of the worker from the means of production and his transformation into a wage-labourer, a seller of the commodity labour-power, he experienced an alienation from himself and from society. The root cause of this alienation, for Marx, was the new form of class society which had developed – capitalism – characterised by its tendency to transform everything into a commodity. For the first time in history the predominant form in which labour was organised was the sale of labour-power as a commodity. Like Durkheim, Marx sought to overcome this state of alienation and create a true human community which would be characterised by a progressive abolition of the division of labour. However, whereas Durkheim had envisaged a conservative and authoritarian corporatism in which the individual would be subordinated to the collectivity, Marx sought the liberation of the individual in exactly the opposite direction. Rather than receiving his moral guidance from authoritative institutions, liberated man would freely come together with his fellows to decide on a course of action. He would dominate social institutions, rather than be subordinate to them. This subordination, which for Durkheim was the solution to the problem of contemporary society, was for Marx yet another symptom of man's alienation; the reification of interpersonal relations into the appearance of things-in-themselves.

Both Marx and Weber were deeply impressed with the productive potentiality of capitalism. Marx, indeed, believed that the inherent growth dynamic of capitalism would create the conditions for its own demise. The fundamental law of capitalist development, for Marx, was its imperative need to accumulate capital. In order to counteract the tendency of the rate of profit to fall in the long run, the ratio of capital to wages had continually to be increased. This proceeded through a series of business cycles which, in the short term, brought with them economic and political crises. The long-term trend was towards the massification of industrial establishments, the homogenisation of the workforce, and its increasing impoverishment. These conditions would produce a constant class struggle between the workers and their employers, and over time, the working class would come to a realisation that their only escape was to overthrow the existing society by seizing hold of the state apparatus, abolishing private property in the means of production, and beginning to form a new social order. The growing concentration and centralisation of capital would itself aid this process.

A great many criticisms have been made of Marx's theory, and we will examine some of them – particularly those relating to the labour theory of value and those specifically dealing with underdeveloped societies – later in this book. And of course later Marxists have modified and altered the theory in a number of ways, not all of them mutually compatible. Indeed such has been the amount of revision and controversy over Marxism that it is now no longer possible to say unequivocally what Marx really meant. One thing must, however, be borne in mind. Marx was writing about capitalism as he observed it in the second half of the nineteenth century, and even if his propositions had been valid for that society (which some historians doubt), capitalism has undergone many changes since. The extent to which these subsequent transformations of capitalism have altered Marx's analysis has been the subject of much controversy: I will examine some of these controversies later in the book.

My present concern is Marx's account of the genesis of modern capitalism. Whereas Weber saw capitalism existing in various forms at all epochs of human society, Marx saw capitalism as a distinct form of society coming into existence only with the bourgeois revolutions of the seventeenth and eighteenth centuries. For Weber, capitalism was defined by an *orientation* towards economic activity, characterised by the rational (that is to say systematic and calculable) pursuit of economic gain by purely economic means. Throughout history there have been groups of men who have been inspired by such capitalist motives. Nevertheless, Weber is in agreement with Marx that it is only with the development of modern Europe that entire societies are dominated by the capitalist impulse. For Marx, capitalism was not defined by the motives or orientations of the capitalists. Whatever they themselves may have believed their motives to be, they were impelled by the logic of the economic system to accumulate capital. Capitalism for Marx was a form of class society structured around a particular way in which men were organised for the production of the necessities of life. It had been preceded in Europe by other forms of class society, in which the relationship between the class or classes of direct producers and the class of non-producers, and the relationship of both classes to the means of production, had been different. Immediately preceding capitalism in Europe had been feudalism, characterised by a direct and unmediated form of exploitation compared with industrial capitalism.

In feudal society, the direct producer, the peasant, had immediate access to land and to tools and implements with which to work the land. He was not separated from the means of production like the worker in capitalism. The feudal peasant was, however, required to work for the lord of the manor for a certain part of the week. This direct and unmediated form of exploitation was held in place by a particular state form. Three elements were central:

1. A complex of laws restricting the mobility of the peasantry, thereby tying them to the lord's estate and making them dependent on him for their livelihood.
2. A decentralised military and judicial apparatus so that each lord had supreme authority within his own domain and maintained his own body of armed retainers; his ties of feudal loyalty to his overlord, and hence eventually to the king, held the polity together on a loose and unstable basis.
3. A unitary and independent church which provided the ideological justification and cement for this structure.

Feudal society was, of course, shot through with contradictions and conflicts and, in any case, was hardly ever to be found in pure form. Some historians have argued that these internal contradictions eventually led to the breakup of feudalism and opened the way for the emergence of capitalism. A number of separate questions are involved.

1. Did feudalism break up because of internal contradictions in the mode of production, or did some external agency cause it to dissolve?
2. If it did break up as a result of internal contradictions, what were they? What was the 'prime mover'?
3. And why did the dissolution of feudalism give rise to capitalism, rather than to some other form of society (Hilton et al., 1976)?

The dating of the transition from feudalism to capitalism is itself a problematic exercise. Maurice Dobb, faced with the need to reconcile the fact that feudalism seems to have declined in the fourteenth century, with the difficulty of dating the rise of capitalism before the sixteenth or seventeenth centuries, argues that there was an intervening period in which the petty commodity mode of production was dominant (Dobb, 1963).

A long period, during which the foundations for the development of capitalism were prepared, intervened between the decline of feudalism proper and the final dominance of the capitalist mode of production. This period saw a process of 'primitive' or 'original' accumulation of capital. A variety of means (plunder, overseas tribute, monopoly profit, enclosures, etc.) were used to bring into being the resources necessary to set capitalism in motion. At the same time, largely as a result of the dispossession of the peasantry through the enclosure movement, a proletariat was created. By the time that the technical advances of the industrial revolution had provided the material basis for the full flowering of industrial capitalism in the eighteenth century, the institutional groundwork was already in existence.

Of course, this notion of an historical hiatus between feudalism and capitalism only makes sense if these modes of production are defined in terms of the nature of the labour process. Implicitly, we have been assuming, along with Dobb, that feudalism is to be defined, primarily, as an economic system based on serfdom, and capitalism as an economic system based on free wage labour. This is, of course, only one element in the definition, but it contrasts sharply with two other ways of defining capitalism and feudalism.

One, the Weberian definition, we have already discussed. The Weberian notion that capitalism is to be defined as a complex of economic attitudes denies any problem of transition in these terms. For Weber, it is not the emergence of capitalism as such which needs to be explained (since capitalism can be found in all historical societies), but rather the specifically *modern* aspects of capitalism. As we have seen, this is to be accounted for in terms of the extension of *rationality* (partly as a secular trend, and partly as an unanticipated consequence of changes in religious doctrines).

The other possible way to define feudalism and capitalism is to identify them, respectively, with natural economy and production for a market. This definition has its origins in Weber, and also in Durkheim's analysis of the *Division of Labour in Society*. It was developed in detail by Henri Pirenne, who argued that after the withdrawal and collapse of the Roman Empire, Western Europe had lapsed into the dark ages of an isolated, stagnant and self-sufficient manorial economy. It was only shaken out of this lethargy, this low-level equilibrium, by the impact of forces external to feudalism. This impact consisted primarily in the revival of trade in the Mediterranean, sparked, in part, by the emergence of the Muslim doctrine (Pirenne, 1936). (Incidentally, it is worth pointing out at this point that this issue of the transition from one mode of production to another, and the definition of the concept of mode of production itself, is one of the central intellectual links between the debate about the development of Western European capitalism and the sociology of development. A curious sense of *déjà vu* was felt by those who witnessed the transposition of this debate to the terrain of the sociology of development in the late 1960s in A. G. Frank's polemics with the Communist Parties of Latin America on the issue of capitalism and feudalism in that continent. More recently, the debate has returned once more to the historiography of the original transition in the West [Wallerstein, 1974; Brenner, 1977; Hindess and Hirst, 1975].)

The two approaches to the definition of capitalism were quite incompatible, as the example of the 'Second Serfdom' in Eastern Europe (and examples from the Third World, such as the agrarian history of Chile) clearly illustrates. What seems to have happened in the areas east of the Elbe, is that the opening up of possibilities to market grain abroad in a major way led to an intensification of direct control over labour rather than the reverse. Instead of increased market orientation leading to proletarianisation of the rural labour force, it led to a re-establishment of serfdom. The reasons for this are to be sought in the state of the market for labour, the distribution of land ownership, and the nature of the class coalition in control of the state. However that may be, the Second Serfdom would be described as a capitalist mode of production by one methodology and as feudalism by the other (Wallerstein, 1974; Anderson, 1974). We are inclined to agree with Ernesto Laclau when he points out that participation in a world capitalist economy ought to be distinguished from the existence of the capitalist mode of production as such (Laclau, 1971).

The market-orientation approach was unsatisfactory, in the opinion of some of the participants in the debate, because it located the principal cause of change *outside* the feudal mode of production. This was at odds with what they held to be the orthodox Marxist belief that every mode of production contained within it internal contradictions which necessarily led to its demise and to the emergence of a new mode of production. It should be noted that Hindess and Hirst, in *Pre-capitalist Modes of Production*, have attempted to argue that the transition from one mode of production does not take place in this way, and that such theoretical enterprises must necessarily incur some element of teleology (Hindess and Hirst, 1975; Foster-Carter, 1978).

But if this was true, that the impetus for change came from within the system, then it was incumbent on the adherents of the labour-process approach to identify these internal contradictions. Moreover, even if this were satisfactorily accomplished, there were some knotty historiographical problems still to be resolved concerning the intervening period between feudalism and capitalism.

There are three principal candidates for the role of internal contradiction or prime mover in feudalism: the struggle between landlord and peasant over land and labour; the rise of towns; and the rise of a centralised absolutist state superseding the decentralised feudal polity.

We will return to the question of the development of the absolutist state in a few pages. Suffice it to say at the moment that the political equilibrium of any system of decentralised fiefs is bound to be precarious. The constant struggle between the component parts of the polity to increase their relative power is likely to produce – via a system of dynastic alliances – some force which is much stronger than the rest. The probability of this faction seizing the state and then reducing the autonomy of the remaining feudal powers must be quite high. Once this centralised state has been created, some of the conditions for a transition to capitalism will have been created. (Though, as we shall see, things are rather more complicated.)

The rise of towns is frequently associated most strongly with the proponents of the 'commercialisation' thesis. Since the early bourgeoisie developed in the towns, these were seen as germs of capitalism existing in the interstices of feudal society. Town and country became the concrete embodiments of the opposition capitalism–feudalism. (The similarity with certain 'dualist' notions of underdevelopment should be noted.)

However, the 'productionist' position also holds that the growth of towns played a role in the transition, though a secondary and indirect one. The 'productionists' tend to give causal primacy to the struggle between lord and peasant over the land. Briefly, this position asserts that the increasing demands of the feudal lords for monetary income meant a constant pressure on the subordinate peasantry to devote more time to demesne production at the expense of their own plots (or to increase the burden of rent – which amounts to the same thing). The ability of the feudal lords to 'squeeze' the peasantry in this manner was by no means absolute. It depended on the scarcity of land, the ability of peasants to flee to the towns, demographic pressures, etc. The persistent theme of peasant revolt throughout the Middle Ages suggests that lordly power was not always absolute.

The very nature of feudalism discouraged any form of technological innovation which might raise productivity rapidly enough to break out of this zero-sum conflict. The persistence of this constant struggle over the appropriation of feudal rent was one of the key factors leading to the rise of the absolutist state. Although the constant need to extract more revenue from the peasantry was by no means the only factor which pushed in the direction of a heightening and centralisation of repressive power, its importance should not be underestimated (Anderson, 1974; Tilly, 1975).

Whatever we might decide about the causes of the breakup of feudalism, it is clear that one of the necessary phases in the development of capitalism was the stage of primitive accumulation of capital. The amount of capital available in the economy had to be expanded rapidly in order for the breakthrough into capitalist growth to occur. This 'free' capital came essentially from two sources. The first was colonial plunder; the sacking of the wealth of the peripheral areas of the world. The second source was the old feudal society itself. The seizure of the vast estates held by the Church, and the dispossession of the land of the peasantry (the enclosure movement) both had the effect of increasing the free capital available and of stimulating a market in land. In addition, the dispossession of the peasantry rendered them landless and set in train the series of events which would lead to the formation of a propertyless proletariat.

The causes of these events were complex, and the process took place over a lengthy period, but whatever the complexities involved, by the mid-eighteenth century a mass of capital was available for investment in industrial expansion. At the same time, the English Civil War of 1640 had set in motion the process of transformation of the state apparatus. The political structures were being adjusted to the needs of capitalist society. Without the prior development of capitalist society, the industrial revolution of the late eighteenth and early nineteenth centuries could never have happened.

The relationship between the transformation of the political structures and the emergence of capitalist relations of production in the economic sphere is a complex one. Any notion that the political system was simply a superstructure which would sooner or later be brought into line with changes in the economic base must be discarded. Some of the origins of the bourgeois nation-states are quite distinct from the causes of the development of the capitalist mode of production. Nevertheless, there were real and intimate connections between the two processes. The absolutist states of late feudalism, though arising primarily as a response to a crisis in and as a defence of the feudal order, served to bridge the way to the development of capitalism. The centralisation of power and the development of large standing armies and systems of national taxes all pointed the way forward (Tilly, 1975). The absolutist state was the setting for a complex symbiosis of elements of the old order and the new (Anderson, 1974). At some times and in certain places the disruptive elements were greater than the forces of cohesion and continuity. In all cases the transition was problematic and fraught with tensions and conflicts.

The debate over the nature of the absolutist state illustrates some of the difficulties of analysis. Perry Anderson has argued, in opposition to the notion that the absolutist state was a state which was independent of classes, balancing a rising bourgeoisie and a declining feudal oligarchy, that it was essentially a *feudal* state. It grew out of the exigency of extracting surplus from a rebellious peasantry. It was, in Anderson's words 'a redeployed and recharged apparatus of feudal domination' (Anderson, 1974, p. 18).

Yet, the absolutist state created the institutional forms appropriate for a capitalist state. In Weberian terms, it signified a tremendous rationalisation of authority. But it only provided the *form* of an advance toward capitalism. What was lacking was that the bourgeoisie should take over the state apparatus for itself. This was eventually to occur, but this struggle for possession of the state (a struggle which would further modify the form of the state apparatus) took on distinct modalities in different countries. In Britain, a slow and drawn-out symbiosis of bourgeoisie and aristocracy enabled the transition to proceed smoothly without major outbreaks of violence. Elsewhere, the transformation of the absolutist state into a modern republic was effected by means of a series of revolutionary episodes, of which the French Revolution of 1789 and the uprisings of 1848 spring most readily to mind.

Despite their different emphases and theoretical orientations, Marx, Weber and Durkheim all agreed that there had been a massive transition in Western Europe which had – however one labelled it – shifted a traditional society to a modern one. This dichotomy was described by the German sociologist, Tönnies, as a shift from *Gemeinschaft* to *Gesellschaft*, from community to association. This image of a transition from community to association underlies the analyses of each of the three thinkers we have discussed above. They all focused, in one way or another, on the breakdown of localised and unmediated units and the emergence of universalistic and impersonal social structures. This dichotomy, and the subsequent search for a source of authoritative moral order, has dominated sociological thinking on the subject ever since.

Talcott Parsons' famous 'pattern variables', the dichotomous sets of alternatives which he claims can be used to characterise all forms of social action, are directly derived from Tönnies' *Gemeinschaft–Gesellschaft* dichotomy. And Parsons' insistence on the primacy for sociological theory of the quest for an explanation of 'the problem of order', of why in a rationalistic and exchange-oriented society there is any kind of social coherence at all, is simply a reassertion of the central concern of the founding fathers (Parsons, 1951). It was with these theoretical lenses that the sociologists of the post-war world were to focus on the problem of underdevelopment in the Third World, as we shall see in the next chapter.

2

Replicating the Transition?

Social science displayed little interest in the societies which now form the Third World until the period after the Second World War. There had, of course, been a great deal in the way of anthropological investigation of parts of some of these societies, but the social structures which were to emerge as the new nations in the 1950s and 1960s had generally not been studied as social wholes. (Some, very limited, exceptions must be made for Latin America, which had been independent since the early nineteenth century.)

When sociology did turn its attention to the underdeveloped world, it was assumed implicitly by a great many researchers that the new nations would follow the same path as that taken by Western European nations, and the theoretical paradigms developed to explain the transition from feudalism to capitalism in Western Europe were imported wholesale, and with very few amendments, into the study of Africa, Asia and Latin America. At first, a simple evolutionary taxonomy of traditional and modern was used.

An important strand in early sociological theory was the attempt to elaborate a theory of social evolution. Although the influence of Darwin was noticeable, other factors were also responsible for the popularity of evolutionary theories in sociology. The expansion of empire was one factor, leading as it did to the elaboration of ideological justifications based on a 'survival of the fittest' theme. But Social Darwinism was not the only form of evolutionary theory.

Men like Herbert Spencer were very much in the mainstream when they attempted to use evolutionary theory to account for the development of human society. With a focus not dissimilar to Durkheim's, Spencer regarded the process of social evolution as one of increasing complexity. He defined evolution as 'a change from a state of relatively indefinite, incoherent homogeneity to a state of relatively definite, coherent heterogeneity' (Carneiro, 1968, p. 122).

The starting point in all these theories of social evolution was an attempt to discover the general trends in the development of all human societies. This usually led to the formulation of a series of stages of development. The notion of a series of stages has been an attractive one for many theorists and continues to exercise appeal today.

There are a number of problems with evolutionary theory. The first concerns the notion of a simple sequence of stages through which all societies pass. There are several difficulties with this, one of which is that the fact of contact between two cultures – diffusion – may modify such a sequence of evolution for one or both societies. One way around this problem is to distinguish between 'specific' and 'general' evolution (Sahlins and Service, 1960) and argue that the sequence of stages only applies to human society as a whole.

A second problem concerns the mechanism which shifts a society from one evolutionary stage to another. What is this mechanism, and why does it operate? As Eisenstadt has noted, 'The first crucial problem concerns the extent to which change from one type of society to another is not accidental or random but, rather, evinces over-all evolutionary or developmental trends' (Eisenstadt, 1968, p. 228).

Then, too, if evolution is seen as a process of progressive differentiation, if the society is not to fall apart there must be a parallel process of re-integration of the increasingly more complex structure. Of course, there need be no teleological necessity for this re-integration to occur. All sorts of failures, blockages and retrocessions may be envisaged and are quite compatible with evolutionary theory.

Despite these problems, theories of social evolution have enjoyed a resurgence of popularity in recent years. The leading figures have been Parsons, Eisenstadt and Bellah, and they have sought to identify a series of 'evolutionary universals' which demarcate stages of social evolution (Eisenstadt, 1964; Parsons, 1964).

Even in the more sophisticated recent versions of the theory, two major problems remain:

1. Can all forms of social change be conceptualised as variants on a differentiation–re-integration process?
2. How is the 'variability of institutionalised solutions to the problems arising from a given level of structural differentiation' to be explained (Eisenstadt, 1968, p. 233)?

It is precisely this range of institutional *variation* which needs to be explained. Evolutionary theory is couched at too general a level to be able to do this, and ought therefore to be abandoned in favour of more historically-oriented theories.

However, despite the obvious problems with evolutionary theory, watered down versions exist in the form of theories of 'stages of growth' and developmental or modernisation theory in general.

The most widespread was the dichotomy 'traditional' – 'modern'. The assumption was that all societies were alike at one stage, in that they were 'traditional', and that eventually they would also pass through the same set of changes as had happened in the West, and become 'modern'. Some of the problems with this vision are mentioned below, but one obvious comment is called for: not all pre-industrial societies are alike. There is a wide range of social structures among them, and there is no reason to assume that the dynamics of change are the same in feudal societies as they are in tribal societies or bureaucratic empires. Moreover, the use of the word 'traditional' conveys a false image of a static equilibrium. Historical research on non-Western societies indicates that that is a totally false impression.

Some theorists elaborated the dichotomy in a more sophisticated way. Drawing on Tönnies' *Gemeinschaft–Gesellschaft* dichotomy, Talcott Parsons had developed his five (or six) pairs of pattern-variables. A follower of his, Bert Hoselitz, attempted to use pattern-variables to describe the process of development, and locate societies along these dichotomies. The fundamental objection to this scheme, to repeat, is the assumption of the validity of a traditional–modern dichotomy (Hoselitz, 1960). In addition, as A. G. Frank has shown in detail, even if one accepted Parsons' pattern-variables as a useful analytic tool, whether one could apply them in a straightforward way to contrast underdeveloped and developed societies is quite dubious (Frank, 1969). He argues that even within the terms of their own theoretical framework, the Parsonians are confronted

;ative evidence. It is by no means clear that developed
are, in fact, predominantly organised in terms of 'modern'
variables, nor that underdeveloped societies are organised
in terms of 'traditional' pattern-variables. But even if one accepts
the Parsonian contention that these sets of pattern-variables do
accurately describe a bipolar situation, the validity of such a dichotomy is itself open to question (Frank, 1969).

Other theories have relied less on this simple dichotomy, and
have, instead, attempted to demarcate a series of stages of development. The most well known of these is the five-stage scheme put
forward by W. W. Rostow in his *Stages of Economic Growth: A
Non-Communist Manifesto* (Rostow, 1960).

Rostow sees the transition from traditional to modern society
taking place through five stages. Modelled explicitly on an analysis
of the British industrial revolution, Rostow's book asserts that all
societies pass through a single, unique sequence of stages. His
analysis centres on the need to increase the rate of capital investment
in a society to the point where growth becomes 'automatic'.

Both Rostow and Hoselitz focus on the need to stimulate the
appearance of an entrepreneurial elite which will lead this development process. This emphasis on entrepreneurship and capital accumulation is the single most pervasive theme in the literature
on economic growth. It always appears as *the* lesson to be learnt
from Western experience and to be mechanically applied to the
rest of the world so that they can repeat the transition.

The emphasis on capital accumulation was by no means confined
to sociologists. Many economists viewed the central problem of
underdevelopment as being some form of low-level equilibrium
trap, a key feature of which was a scarcity of capital.

While the application of the paradigm of endogenous change
based on the experience of the West, as applied by modernisation
and development theorists, focused on values, capital and entrepreneurship, a similar paradigm focusing on similar factors was
in vogue among many Marxists. The key question revolved around
the role of the bourgeoisie in a supposed transition from feudalism
to capitalism in the countries of the Third World. This rather
crude and mechanical version of Marxism, heavily influenced by
the long night of Stalinism, progressed no further in theoretical
terms than the debates engaged in by the Russian revolutionaries
at the turn of the century. Corresponding to the notions of 'tradi-

tional' and 'modern', Marxists used two categories, 'feudal' and 'capitalist', and debated whether it was possible to 'skip stages', combine them, or whether a unilinear sequence of invariable stages of development had to be followed. Third World countries were classified as feudal, as capitalist, or perhaps as semi-feudal–semi-capitalist (a formulation which, precisely because of its absence of theoretical rigor, provided great flexibility in action). These debates were not always useless, and as we shall see in the discussion of the work of Andre Gunder Frank, it may sometimes be necessary to analyse Third World societies in precisely those terms.

The most common position, in fact, was to argue that the societies of the Third World were semi-feudal, semi-capitalist. This formulation, in all its ambiguity, might mean several things. It might simply be an ideological obfuscation, a blurring of the image of reality to force it into a predetermined doctrinal mould. Or it might refer to a state of transition, characterised by complex class alliances. Or thirdly, it might indicate some form of dualism.

In its original usage, this term was employed by those who believed that Third World societies were composed of a modern sector and a traditional sector. Some extreme versions suggested that these two sectors were pretty much watertight compartments with very few interrelations between them. This is implausible, and some writers, of whom A. G. Frank is the most notable, have suggested that there exist, in fact, a whole series of mechanisms whereby the modern sector exploits the traditional sector and thereby generates underdevelopment in the traditional sector. Frank goes so far as to argue that one cannot even properly talk of two distinct sectors; rather, there is a continual chain of exploitative relations between the most advanced and the most backward sectors of a society.

It is doubtful if either of these extreme versions can be accepted. Clearly one *can* distinguish modern and traditional (or informal) sectors which have some degree of autonomy from each other. Equally clearly, there do exist all sorts of connections between the two sectors. Thus, the thesis of the co-existence of traditional and modern sectors, or of feudal and capitalist modes of production, is not an unreasonable one. However, the question of how these two sectors are related (or articulated, to use a currently fashionable phrase) remains unresolved. But before we can analyse the complex articulation of modes of production (why always complex, why never simple?) we must first look at the different ways in which 'mode of production' is employed.

For some writers, such as Hindess and Hirst, the term appears to carry no empirical referent whatsoever, and it is difficult to see what function it would have in any kind of historical investigation. (This has been tacitly admitted by Hindess and Hirst in their auto-critique (Hindess and Hirst, 1977).) Others, such as Norman Long, seem to use the term to describe certain kinds of occupational roles. Thus, a peasant who at times works as a serf on a hacienda and at other times employs wage labour on his private plot is described as participating in two or more modes of production (Long, 1975).

Related to this usage is the notion that the enterprise is the basic unit of a mode of production. Thus, a society may be composed of capitalist enterprises, enterprises based on slave labour (slave mode of production), artisanal enterprises, etc. In this analysis, social classes are formed by the political coalescence of these economic roles. There is no immediate or direct connection between the set of contradictions generated by the economic structure and the process of class formation and political conflict.

A quite different notion of the term 'mode of production' is to use it to describe a social totality, a structured whole, which embodies a class structure and a set of political institutions which form a unity with the economic 'base'. Often, the empirical referent of mode of production will be the national society (in which case there is no question of co-existence, except as a temporary phenomenon of transition). Hamza Alavi tends to use the term in this way (Alavi, 1975). Immanuel Wallerstein also believes that 'mode of production' denotes a systematic whole, but argues that there is only one level of wholeness, that of the world system (Wallerstein, 1974). However, it also seems possible to argue that systematic wholes may be formed at a level lower than that of the national society. It is not implausible that, at a regional level, a distinct form of economy could give rise to a specific set of social classes and even to local political institutions. Both at the political level and at the economic level, there would be some form of institutional link with the larger society. As an example of this form of articulation of modes of production, one might mention the plantations of the Brazilian Northeast. Here, a form of economic organisation distinct from the rest of the nation existed under the protective mantle of a system of political clientelism which preserved some measure of local autonomy. This political apparatus 'articulated' two modes of production.

But, however one cares to use the notion of a complex articulation of modes of production, the question still remains, are we talking about a transition from feudalism to capitalism, however complex?

If this is the case, three fallacious assumptions are entailed. The first is that all the societies of the underdeveloped world could reasonably be described as 'feudal'. Some societies may have borne a certain resemblance to European feudalism, but for the majority, there could be little doubt that their social structures were quite dissimilar in many ways and therefore the inner dynamic and internal contradictions of these societies were not the same as those of European feudalism.

The second fallacious assumption is that all societies progress inevitably through a single, fixed evolutionary scheme. There is no real basis in fact for such an assumption of unilinear evolution, and at best it should have been treated as simply one possible hypothesis.

In any case, even if this evolutionary approach is correct, it depends on the third assumption in order for it to be operationalised. This third assumption is that the process of social change is essentially endogenous. The model derived from the experience of Western Europe presupposed a closed system, with some catalytic change occurring within it and then triggering off a sequence of changes which would produce a transition from traditional to modern. (Some theorists, as we saw in the discussion of the Marxist debate on the transition from feudalism to capitalism, argued that even in Western Europe the changes had occurred largely as a result of influences from outside the system. Nevertheless, the dominant paradigmatic assumption continued to be that of endogenous change.) This assumption of endogenous change is clearly inadmissible for the countries of the Third World. Their incorporation into the process of rapid social change occurred, in fact, as a direct result of their contact with the expanding societies of Western Europe (and later the USA), and most of the processes of change which have occurred in these societies have been in direct response to the impact of the West.

Once all three of these assumptions are dropped, then the applicability of the model of social transformation derived from the histori-

cal experience of the West can only be applied with serious modifications. However, while it cannot be applied directly, it can provide
the starting point for a more comprehensive theory of social change
which will be able to embrace the process of transformation both
in the original centre and in the new societies of the periphery.
Rather than throw out the baby with the bathwater, and deny
that anything can be learnt from the historical experience of the
West, it would be more profitable systematically to compare that
experience with the changes that are currently taking place in
the Third World and, where relevant, explicate the causal links
between changes occurring at the centre of the world system and
changes occurring in the periphery.

From the point of view of Marxist theory, one response has
been to attempt to develop a global theory of modes of production.
This enterprise involves the creation of an exhaustive *list* of all
modes of production, a theory of their dynamics, and a theory
of their interrelationships (theory of transition and theory of articulation). However, the question of how one might begin to draw
up such a list is not amenable to any kind of simple solution.

To assume that from an arbitrary and given set of theoretical
variables one can generate such a list, without reference to events
in the real world, is to accept an epistemological position which
is hard to distinguish from the worst kinds of scholastic idealism.
An alternative approach, to construct a general theory after a
series of tentative historical explorations using 'mode of production
analysis' would seem more likely to produce results. But the day
when such a general theory is available is far off. For the moment
we must be content with more middle-range theories.

Given the predominant evolutionary paradigm, in order to
explain why the West had developed and the rest of the world
had not, scholars were driven to seek for some 'missing factor'
which was absent in the societies of the Third World and would
account for their failure to achieve economic growth. A variety
of contenders for the role of 'missing factor' were suggested.

The most obvious was the lack of capital. The societies of the
Third World had failed to develop because they were too poor;
there simply was not enough wealth available to build up the
kind of capital base necessary for economic development. This
may, indeed, have been true of some societies, but it did not
explain what had happened in countries like China and India,

where there had been ancient civilisations with enormous wealth. Nor did it explain the failure to develop of societies like the West Indies from which vast quantities of riches were transferred to the metropolis throughout the modern period. More institutionally-oriented explanations had to be elaborated, which focused on phenomena like capital markets, rather than the sheer amount of wealth as such.

Related to this were theories which suggested that the missing factor was not capital as such but rather entrepreneurship. Here the theories moved increasingly into the realm of ideological fantasy, returning to nineteenth-century ideological justifications of inequality which had focused on the exceptional and personal qualities of the individual entrepreneur – the nearest thing to a hero bourgeois society had produced. Although this belief – that entrepreneurship was one of the missing factors (or perhaps the main missing factor) – recurs in many explanations, two theories may be singled out for a closer look.

True to the nature of the theme, both of the theorists we shall examine propose primarily psychological explanations. McClelland, in a crude and *simpliste* vulgar misinterpretation of Weber, argues that if the Protestant ethic caused economic growth in the West, then some analogous phenomenon must be sought elsewhere in order to achieve economic growth. What lay behind Weber's Protestant ethic, McClelland argues, was a personality trait, the need to achieve (N-ach, for short). Modern psychological tests could uncover this trait, and determine its incidence in any given population. In order to provide some kind of evidence for this proposition, McClelland sought to show that there existed a correlation between periods of economic advance in societies and the incidence of N-achievement in their populations (McClelland, 1961).

Two kinds of criticism may be made. In the first place, an internal criticism of the adequacy of McClelland's evidence may be advanced (Kilby, 1971). This will not be attempted here, since my concern is with more general issues. However, irrespective of whether or not McClelland's evidence is internally consistent – in that there does not appear to be any correlation between a set of characteristics which he identifies as N-achievement and periods of economic growth – more general criticisms may be levelled at his theory. To begin with, McClelland conflates different kinds of economic growth and transformation, thereby obscuring the important differences between the kinds of societies involved. In the second place, his theory is psychologically reductionist, since it attempts to explain a sociological phenomenon (that is, the transformation of one type of social structure into another) purely in terms of psychological variables.

Everet Hagen's theory at least avoids this pitfall, though it too has serious defects. Hagen argues that changes in childhood socialisation patterns may produce a change in personality types which has repercussions for social change. The sequence of events goes something like this: some disturbing event produces a shock and withdrawal of status respect for some elite group who are displaced from power. The immediate psychological reaction is retreatism and a period of withdrawal. During this period child-rearing patterns will alter. Out of this will come a reaction and the emergence of values conducive to economic growth (Hagen, 1962).

Although this theory is similar to McClelland's in that it sees economic growth as the end point of a causal chain going from childhood socialisation and personality factors to entrepreneurship, it has the merit of attempting to locate the source of this characterological change in some shift in the social structure. However, it is quite difficult to operationalise the theory. From the examples given by Hagen himself, the withdrawal of status respect seems to be identified with any plausible trauma in a period between 40 and 400 years prior to economic growth. At times Hagen talks about a period of withdrawal of 'several centuries' (Hagen, 1962, p. 378). And yet in another example, McCarthyism in the United States is explained as a response to the 1930s depression. Why not the trauma of 1776?

Hagen's explanation is, in fact, overelaborate. There is no need to take the detour of psychological reductionism to account for most processes of structural change. It is simply redundant.

Of course Hagen, like most theorists working within a modernisation paradigm, is not explicitly concerned with structural change per se. But this is precisely what the question of development and underdevelopment is about. It is not simply a matter of societies being different merely in matters of degree; they are different in kind, and to explain the transition from one kind of society to another we must deal with structural change. As is argued throughout this book, such structural changes are best explained by reference to the changing relationships between social classes.

Generally speaking, it is possible to analyse these changing interclass relationships without delving too deeply into the complexities of individual psychology.

Barrington Moore's book, *The Social Origins of Dictatorship and Democracy*, offers a good illustration of a structural explanation (Moore, 1966). Moore's work, which is an excellent piece of historically informed theorising, attempts a structural explanation of the various paths to modern society. Moore sees three routes to modernisation: the classical bourgeois revolutions which give rise to democracies; revolution from above, by a reactionary alliance between a landed aristocracy and a modernising elite, which gives rise to variants of fascism; and revolution from below, in which a peasant revolt becomes the vehicle for a Communist-inspired drive towards modernity. The central structural variables which Moore identifies, and which determine which path is followed, have to do with the nature of the class structure and, in particular, with the response of the landed upper class to commercialisation of agriculture.

Whether or not the theory is adequate in its own terms – and it must be stressed that in terms of historical and structural explanation, Moore provides an excellent analysis – this theory is only applicable to the big and relatively self-contained societies which Moore deals with: England, France, Germany, Russia, the United States, Japan, China and India. It is a model of endogenous change, and as Moore himself notes, it is not capable of dealing with small societies which are subject to external influences (Moore, 1966, p. xiii). Even in Moore's own treatment, the case of India is highly problematic, since this is a society which has always been subject to massive external influences. Although the societies which Moore works with are indeed some of the most important societies in the contemporary world, the vast mass of Third World countries are excluded from his analysis by the simple fact that he cannot deal with exogenous influences.

This tendency toward endogenous explanation is widespread and seriously limits many otherwise excellent analyses. For example, Helio Jaguaribe's interesting typology of developmental projects shares with Barrington Moore's book a tendency towards an exclusion of exogenous variables. Jaguaribe identifies several types of society. These societies have chosen from among a limited range of operational political developmental models. Jaguaribe identifies nine such models, which may occasionally be combined. Of course, the choice of model is severely constrained by the type of society. Jaguaribe's main interest is in the three specifically developmental models, national capitalism, state capitalism and developmental socialism (Jaguaribe, 1973).

National capitalism involves the 'modernizing sectors of the national bourgeoisie and the middle class in alliance with the proletariat and with the support of the mobilized peasants versus traditional and consular sectors of the bourgeoisie and middle class, their foreign bosses, partners, and allies and antimodernizing rural sectors' (Jaguaribe, 1973, p. 282). It operates by a 'combination of state and private entrepreneurial action' and under a neo-Bismarckian leadership.

State capitalism involves the 'modernizing sector of the middle class, with full support of urban and rural masses versus traditional patrician elite and their consular allies in the bourgeoisie and middle class'. The private sector is not suppressed, but the state plays a greater role in the economy. Power is usually exercised by forms of 'authoritarian co-optation combined with mass plebiscites' (Jaguaribe, 1973, pp. 282–3).

Finally, with developmental socialism, 'the intelligentsia of the counterelite organised in a revolutionary, well-disciplined party, with support of party-controlled urban and rural masses' employs the state to maximise economic growth (Jaguaribè, 1973, p. 283).

It will be seen that these three models lie along two continua: free enterprise–state ownership and political democracy–authoritarianism. They also differ in terms of the class alliance in control of the state.

Some attempt is made to incorporate exogenous variables into the analysis by writers, like Gerschenkron, who stress some of the advantages of 'backwardness' (Gerschenkron, 1962). According to Gerschenkron, one of the advantages which accrues to a backward country is that it can skip stages in technological development by importing relatively advanced technology without having to pay the costs of developing it. Nevertheless, once having made this observation, it is not at all clear what effects this has on the social structure of the country in question. And, in any event, we are still left with a stages theory. However, whether we can ever do without some kind of stages theory may be doubted.

The Marxist equivalent of Gerschenkron's theory of the advantages of backwardness is to be found in the theory put forward earlier by Trotsky and Parvus, under the name of 'permanent revolution' (Trotsky, 1931). Trotsky emphasised the way in which a backward country like Russia imported modern technology and large-scale enterprises, and was thus able to develop a substantial modern industrial proletariat even while most of the countryside remained steeped in archaic agriculture.

This uneven and combined development meant that when the bourgeoisie came to push for a greater share in state power and came into conflict with the landed aristocracy, it would have to call on the industrial working class as an ally in its fight. However, since the bourgeoisie was relatively weak and the working class was relatively strong, the bourgeoisie would be inclined to waver and temporise with the landed aristocracy rather than run the risk of a proletarian revolution. Meanwhile, the working class, first as an ally of the bourgeoisie and then increasingly as an autonomous actor, would put forward its own political demands and would, when the bourgeoisie began to waver, assume the leadership of the movement and push the revolution forward beyond the bourgeois stage into the stage of the proletarian revolution.

Like all the other stage models considered up to now, Trotsky's analysis omits discussion of changes in the context of change. Since change is very rarely endogenous, the context of change must somehow be incorporated into the model itself. How a society moves from one stage to another will depend not only on the internal dynamics of the transition, but also on how that society is inserted into the world system at a particular point in the development of that system. That is, a prior task must always be a periodisation of the world system, and an analysis of the way in which any given society is articulated with that world system. Only then can we begin to specify how the external environment (if indeed such a distinction makes much sense) affects the internal processes of social change.

However, it is important that the argument presented in this chapter not be misunderstood. To assert that one cannot study processes of social change without putting them in their context does not imply that the only important factor is the external context itself. Some radical dependency theorists have at times inclined toward a one-sided emphasis on the determining role of the world market, and have seen developments within Third World countries as mere reflections of, or responses to, exogenous changes. Such purely exogenously determined models of change are as inadequate as the purely endogenous models criticised in this chapter. The task – and it is by no means an easy one – is to combine both endogenous and exogenous factors in a single integrated theory.

3
Internal Obstacles

At the same time that the theories discussed in the previous chapter were being rapidly elaborated and nearly as rapidly discarded, economists were focusing more attention on the details of economic development. A series of specific debates and controversies sprang up, as the complexities of the process began to be recognised. This body of work increasingly led in the direction of breaking out of the old endogenous paradigm which had bogged down sociological theorising.

One of the key agencies involved in this new approach to development economics was the United Nations Economic Commission for Latin America (ECLA), under the direction of the Argentine economist Raúl Prebisch. It is not surprising that the relatively most advanced part of the underdeveloped world should be the scene for some of the most important theoretical developments in the early post-war period.

The key breakthrough in rupturing the old paradigm was the focus on the fact that Latin America had developed as an integral part of the expanding world economy. The theorists of ECLA asserted that there was an immediate and direct link between changes in the industrialised countries of the centre and the underdeveloped countries of the periphery. ECLA argued that the period from the late nineteenth century until the middle of the twentieth century had been a period of development oriented towards the outside. Latin America had taken on the role of supplier of raw materials and foodstuffs for the industrial nations and had, in return, imported manufactured products. According to conventional theories of international trade, such a division of labour, following the contours of natural advantage, worked to the benefit of both partners. However, the theory made certain crucial assumptions about the mobility of the factors of production. It assumed that the factors of production would be rewarded according to their marginal productivity, and that this would be influenced by the relative abundance of any particular factor. It assumed more or less perfect markets for the factors of production. ECLA argued that, since the factor markets were far from perfect, the system of international trade operated against the interests of the Latin American nations. The ECLA argument focused on the terms of trade. They argued – and this is a matter of some controversy – that the available evidence showed that the terms of trade had been moving against the Latin American nations since about 1870. This meant that every quantum of Latin American exports brought in return a smaller and smaller quantum of imports of manufactured goods from the industrial centre (Baer, 1969).

As originally put forward, the ECLA thesis really consisted of two arguments which were often presented together and sometimes conflated. The first argument focused on the role of demand. It asserted that the income elasticity of demand for raw materials and foodstuffs was less than one. That is, any increase in the income of consumers would result in an increase in consumption of raw materials and foodstuffs, but not to the same degree; so that as people became richer, they would spend a smaller and smaller proportion of their income on raw materials and foodstuffs, even if their absolute levels of consumption rose.

This was due to three factors: (1) Engel's law stated that the income elasticity of food was less than one, so that as people's incomes rose, they spent a smaller proportion of their incomes on foodstuffs; (2) agricultural protection policies in the industrial nations would further discriminate against imported foodstuffs; and (3) technological advances would diminish the demand for raw materials as synthetic substitutes were discovered. All this would mean that the income elasticity of imports at the centre would be less than one. The same sort of argument suggested that the income elasticity of demand for manufactured goods (the imports of the Latin American countries) would be greater than one, so that as incomes rose, people would spend increasingly larger proportions of their incomes on manufactured goods. Therefore, the income elasticity of Latin America's imports would be greater than one. This imbalance in the income elasticities of imports in the centre and the periphery would mean a long-run decline in the terms of trade and hence a reduced capacity on the part of the Latin American nations to import from the industrial West.

The second argument put forward by ECLA had to do with wage levels in the two areas. In an early version of what later came to be known as a theory of unequal exchange, ECLA claimed that the gains from productivity increases were unequally distributed between centre and periphery. By the late nineteenth century, so the argument went, productivity increases at the centre were matched by increases in wages as a result of trade union pressure. In consequence, manufacturers raised their prices. This was possible owing to the monopolisation of the economy. In the countries of the periphery, however, the mass of available labour meant that there was a highly competitive labour market and wages hardly rose above subsistence levels. Hence, increases in productivity were not matched by increases in wages, and there was therefore no tendency for the prices of the products of the periphery (food and raw materials) to rise.

In support of this thesis, ECLA claimed that whenever this pattern of outward-oriented development was interrupted by war or world economic depression, there was a spurt of industrial development in Latin America. These spurts came to an end as soon as the economic ties between centre and periphery were re-established and the pattern of development towards the outside was resumed. Whereas these early spurts of industrialisation had not been planned and had arisen as *ad hoc* responses to a rapid decline in the capacity to import, ECLA argued that the only realistic policy for Latin American countries was to adopt a deliberate policy of fostering this sort of import-substitution industrialisation and turn away from a policy of development towards the outside in favour of a policy of development towards the inside. To do this, certain structural obstacles to the expansion of the domestic market had to be removed, and ECLA moved on to an analysis of the nature of these obstacles.

In principle, ECLA's arguments were equally applicable to other Third World countries, though the specific nature of the obstacles in the way of expansion of the internal market might vary considerably from one part of the world to another. It should be noted, in addition, that whether or not ECLA was correct in its analysis of the supposed tendency for the terms of trade to decline, its analyses and recommendations were accepted by many policy-makers and they acted on the assumption that these trends did exist. In a sense, therefore, the correctness or otherwise of ECLA's analysis of the terms of trade is now a largely irrelevant issue.

The historical experience of the Latin American economies appeared to provide historical evidence for this theory (though some studies, such as Warren Dean's, suggest that the evidence for an inverse relationship between links to the world economy and economic growth is not entirely clearcut). In the post-war world, ECLA proposed that these early and unplanned beginnings should be systematised and that policy measures be deliberately adopted to foster import-substitution industrialisation. A package of measures was proposed. It included a series of protectionist measures such as tariffs for domestic industry, careful manipulation of exchange rates to achieve the same effect, and a series of measures to broaden the internal market. This meant simultaneously an attack on the old landed exporting oligarchies via a process of land reform and export diversification, and a redistribution of income to increase consumer demand for relatively low-priced manufactured goods.

In political terms, this strategy was seen as an alliance of nearly all social classes against the landed oligarchy, which was held responsible for the lack of economic progress. It was argued that the political dominance of this landed oligarchy, with its huge and inefficient latifundia, producing mainly for export, prevented the kinds of economic reforms that were necessary for economic growth. Change therefore could not be piecemeal; a structural transformation of the economy was necessary. The peasantry, once freed from the oppressive and inefficient latifundio system, would produce more foodstuffs and their incomes would increase. This would increase their demand for domestically-produced manufactured goods, thereby stimulating national industry. Deliberate state intervention in the economy would foster the creation of new industrial enterprises, and the industrial bourgeoisie and/or the urban middle classes would take over state power from the landed oligarchy. The industrial working class would benefit from increased employment, and the policy of maximising consumer demand by redistributing income would ensure that they would benefit in real terms from economic growth.

In many ways, this analysis was similar to the arguments put forward by the Communist Party, which had for many years argued that revolutionaries should support the 'progressive national bourgeoisie' in its struggle to remove the last vestiges of feudalism and imperialist domination, and modernise the economy. In both versions, an isolated but still powerful landed oligarchy stood opposed to 'the people' as the defender of the old order. Both strategies called for a broad alliance of all social classes under the leadership of the progressive sector of the bourgeoisie. (In some of the writings on Latin America, the term 'bourgeoisie' drops out of sight and is replaced by the phrase 'middle class' or 'middle sector'. Despite the obvious ideological intent, and the confusions to which the implicit equation of 'middle class' and bourgeoisie give rise, the analyses were remarkably similar.) Common to both strategies was a conception of the problem of underdevelopment as consisting primarily in an interlocking set of (largely internal) obstacles. Once these were removed, then industrialisation and increases in real welfare could proceed without major difficulty. These obstacles were identified, as we have said, at the political level, as the political domination of a reactionary landed upper class, and in economic terms as the perpetuation of an obsolete landholding system which had been suited to a pattern of development towards the outside, but which was a brake on development oriented towards the expansion of the domestic market.

An unusual configuration of events led the United States to adopt the policy proposals implied in the ECLA critique. Land reform, and the support of the 'progressive' sectors of the industrial bourgeoisie, became the key elements in the new strategy for change. By the early 1960s, in the years following the Cuban revolution, the Kennedy administration came to believe that the glaring social inequalities and injustices of Latin America might easily spark off other outbursts of revolution on the continent. The whole of Latin America might become a war zone, with the Andes as the Sierra Maestra of the continent. (This vision was also held by many supporters of the Cuban revolution, cf. Guevara and Debray.) This analysis was extremely simplistic and short-sighted. Within a few years, observers were stressing the uniqueness of the Cuban situation, with the implicit conclusion that Latin America as a whole was not teetering on the brink of armed insurrection in the early 1960s. Nevertheless, since key policy-makers evidently had such a vision of the world, they acted on that vision. So the weight of the United States was also thrown into the alliance against the oligarchies. Not simply for moral reasons; mainly, rather,

because it was felt that certain concessions and reforms were imperative to head off imminent revolution, and the landed oligarchies
were an obstacle to this. At the same time, the United States
began an intensive programme of reorganising the armies of Latin
America so that they could deal efficiently with guerrilla threats
and extinguish foci of discontent before a Vietnam-sized conflag-
ration took hold.

This political alliance had, in the 1930s, appeared in Latin
America in the form of populism, and in the new states of Africa
and Asia frequently took the form, in the post-war world, of varieties
of 'national socialism' – African socialism, Burmese socialism, etc.
We will discuss how these poly-class movements organised the masses
politically to provide a power base for intra-elite struggles in later
chapters.

However, by the mid-1960s Latin America's experience with
import-substituting industrialisation had not been entirely satisfactory. In the first place, dependency on a single export commodity
had not been broken. This was shown most dramatically in the
case of the Cuban revolution itself.

The reform programme which Fidel Castro's 26 July movement
sought to implement immediately after their seizure of power in
1959 was an almost classical version of ECLA's proposals. The
Cubans wanted to break away from the centuries-long stranglehold
which sugar had had on the island, and one of their first moves
was an attempt to diversify agriculture. They also implemented
a rapid agrarian reform, began a programme of rapid industrialisation, redistributed income and broke their ties with the United
States. All these measures fitted in well with ECLA's prescriptions.
But by 1963, the Cuban leadership had changed course, in the
face of mounting economic difficulties. Some of these were, of
course, due to US hostility, and in particular to the economic
blockade. But a great many of the problems which plagued the
Cuban leadership resulted from the economic policy itself. Both
the redistribution of income and the rapid industrial expansion
placed a great strain on the productive capacity of the country.
In particular, there was an increased demand for imports of raw
materials, spare parts and capital goods for the new industries.
And the diversification of agriculture, carried out to the detriment
of sugar, meant that the foreign exchange which was needed to
pay for these imports was not forthcoming. The crucial fact that,

for many underdeveloped countries, the export sector functioned as a quasi-capital goods sector, had been entirely neglected.

Moreover, in the short run, import-substitution of manufactured imports did not lessen the need for imports; rather, the type of imports changed from consumer goods to manufacturers goods. This industrialisation by stages meant there was now even less flexibility in import requirements, since any interruption in the flow of raw materials and parts for domestic industry had profound consequences for the economy as a whole. As a result, by 1963, Cuba returned to the production of sugar for export in a big way, and in order to ensure stable markets for her exports (as well as sources for imports for her industrial development) turned to the Soviet Union to replace the United States as her major trading partner. (Of course, there were other profound differences, but the initial daydreams of autarchic development had been firmly squashed.)

This experience was repeated elsewhere in Latin America, with two major differences. In the first place, the reforms were by no means quite so thoroughgoing as they had been in Cuba, and there were many compromises with the landed oligarchy. In the second place, the continued openness of these economies to the United States meant that when tariff barriers were raised to make manufactured imports expensive, US-based manufacturing companies simply set up subsidiaries in the Latin American countries themselves. This did mean, of course, that industry was now located within the geographical boundaries of the underdeveloped countries, but it did not mean that the industry was Latin American in ownership. The importance of this distinction will be discussed below.

The ease with which the foreign corporations were able to take advantage of this set of policies designed to stimulate industrial growth points to a relatively weak part of the theoretical framework then in vogue. Although the central part of the explanation of the backwardness of the periphery had been the exploitative relationship between it and the centre, apart from the supposed tendency of the terms of trade to decline, the mechanisms of this exploitative relationship had not been explored in detail. In ECLA's view, foreign capital could play an important and useful role in the process of economic growth, and was therefore to be welcomed. It was only the theories of imperialism stemming from Marxism which questioned the validity of this assumption, and it was at this point that ECLA chose to stop its own analysis. Rather than turn towards a detailed examination of the operation of the various mechanisms of imperialism, ECLA, and the school of sociological analysis linked loosely with it, turned their attention inward in a search for the obstacles to development.

A common metaphor was that of vicious circles of poverty, or low-level equilibrium traps. It was argued that, in a great many areas of life in underdeveloped countries, the chains of causation perpetuated poverty and prevented progress. What was needed, accordingly, was some kind of sharp rupture which would reverse the chains of causation and turn the vicious circles into 'virtuous' circles. While by no means underestimating the difficulties of doing this, this view of the causes of the persistence of underdevelopment was inherently optimistic: a sharp rupture at any given time would set in motion a self-sustaining process of growth; all that was needed was this single sharp rupture (Myrdal, 1957).

There were a number of problems with the attempt at import-substitution industrialisation. In addition to the increasingly rigid import requirement, there were a series of problems having to do with market size. The technology available to the underdeveloped countries was that developed in the advanced nations where labour was expensive and capital relatively cheap. In the Third World, on the contrary, cheap labour was abundant and capital was expensive. The technologies available tended to involve massive outlays on capital, and employed very few people. Little research was, or is, done on types of technology appropriate to the factor endowments of the majority of Third World countries.

At the same time the scale of operation of many of these technologies was such that the smallest available unit (say a steel mill) was often much larger than was required for the market size of the underdeveloped country. This meant that if such a plant were installed then it would work at less than full capacity and real resources would have been wasted. The obvious solution to this – a common market and regional planning agreements between groups of Third World countries – is extremely difficult to achieve in practice, given the division of the world into nation-states which do not conform to 'natural' economic regions.

Another set of problems had to do with the demand profile of the underdeveloped countries and the baskets of goods actually in demand. If the bulk of the population was very poor, then much of the demand for manufactured goods would, in fact, come from a small number of very wealthy people. This section of the population would have expensive luxury tastes which were not conducive to the development of a sound economic base, and in any case had a high import content. Sound and broad-based economic advance would mean income redistribution and with it, a change in the demand profile of Third World countries. Instead of large, luxury automobiles, buses and trucks would be manufactured. However, the entire productive structure of the multinational corporations is geared to the manufacture of precisely these high-income commodities. And this is backed up with a massive apparatus of advertising and mass communication which means that, when people in the Third World manifest their free choice in a market place dominated by the values of the countries of advanced capitalism, they do so by purchasing precisely those commodities which are dysfunctional for balanced economic growth.

This set of reasons meant that the policies designed to achieve rapid industrialisation in Latin America were not very successful. Most attempts at industrialisation via the substitution of imports led to increasing balance of payments problems, increased foreign penetration of the economy, increasing unemployment, widening rather than narrowing income differentials, greater vulnerability of the economy to cyclical movements, a continuing dependency on the export of a limited range of raw materials or agricultural products, and limited and fluctuating industrial growth. Above all, it was increasingly clear that the mass of the population was not participating in the benefits of economic growth. If anything, they were getting poorer and poorer.

This disenchantment with the magic formula of ECLA occurred at the same time in Latin America as a new and radically different model of economic growth was being tried out in practice. The clearest example is the so-called 'Brazilian model'.

Brazil, in the period up to 1964, had been a good example of the Import Substitution Industrialisation (ISI) policies. However, by the 1960s it appeared to many observers that the Brazilian economy was experiencing a serious crisis. This falling off in the growth rate, with its attendant inflation and balance of payments problems was interpreted by some as the 'exhaustion of ISI' (Ellis, 1969). It was argued that the 'easy' phase of the substitution of manufactured goods had been nearly completed in Brazil, and that a new stage had to be embarked upon (Furtado, 1965).

This economic crisis was superimposed on a political crisis, as the populist president, Goulart, sought a way out of the economic impasse. The political crisis stemmed from the specific way in which the political tensions of Brazilian development had been controlled in the 1930s and 1940s. The decay of the old agrarian oligarchies and the rise of new agrarian coffee capitalists based in São Paulo and linked with the newer sectors of the industrial bourgeoisie had meant changes in the nature of the state. Under considerable middle-class pressure, the old patrician ruling class made way for a more active state which could effectively represent the interests of the new bourgeoisie. The New State (*Estado Nôvo*) of Getulio Vargas represented an uneasy compromise which oversaw this period of transition. In the post-war period a limited opening up of the system took place. However, this popular mobilisation soon threatened to get out of hand and outstrip the capacity of the existing political institutions to handle it. The president, Goulart, was caught between the increasingly vociferous mobilised populist masses on the one hand, and the increasingly alarmed established interests on the other. His dithering in this situation merely served to exacerbate the crisis and bring it to a head.

In the end he was overthrown by a military *coup d'état*, and it was left to the military government to take the measures which would evolve into the 'Brazilian model'. The initial measures consisted of an orthodox programme of economic stabilisation. Wages were reduced, there was budgetary restraint, and in the ensuing recession, the rate of inflation fell to manageable levels. Some observers believed that Brazil had entered a period of profound stagnation, and this belief found convincing support from those radical theorists like Baran and Frank who argued that capitalism in the underdeveloped world was incompatible with economic growth of any but the most superficial kind.

These beliefs about the secular stagnation of Brazilian society were brought into question by the spectacular revival of the economy after 1967. In the years immediately after 1967 – and before the world recession of 1973 induced a slowdown in Brazil – the Brazilian economy grew at a phenomenal rate (9 per cent p.a.). This growth may be attributed to a reversal of the ISI model of income distribution. Rather than make the distribution of income more equitable, there was a concentration of income, with most of the benefits of growth going to the top 20 per cent of income earners. This sector provided the market for modern consumer durables: automobiles, televisions, washing machines, etc., while the remaining 80 per cent participated in the 'miracle' only as producers, and not as consumers. (This duality could be exaggerated.) The expansion of this market was brought about by a massive inflow of foreign capital attracted by the relatively low wages and even more by the controlled and stable labour movement, as well as by deliberate government incentives. In addition to attracting foreign capital and creating a favourable investment climate through the use of state repression of the labour movement, the Brazilian state intervened directly in the economy to build up the economic infrastructure and capital goods sector, so that the multinationals could invest in the profitable and dynamic sectors of the economy (consumer durables) without major problems. Meanwhile, local capital supplemented the activities of the multinationals by remaining in or moving into the non-durable consumer goods sector, and by supplying the multinationals with components and essential services.

The economic dynamic was further stimulated by a push towards the export of manufactured products to other underdeveloped countries. In some ways this looked like the beginning of a role for Brazil as a kind of sub-imperialism; a kind of forward staging-post for the penetration of the markets of other underdeveloped countries. This process was not, however, without its contradictions and tensions.

It meant, in the first place, the installation and maintenance of a political regime which intensified and developed to a new height the authoritarian tendencies of the state apparatus. (The class nature of this state apparatus, and the way in which the military with their relative independence from the Brazilian bourgeoisie were able to mediate the links between the local and international factions of capital, are detailed below in Chapter 9.) The exclusion of the mass of the citizenry from political participation, the crushing of the left, the restrictions placed on the labour movement, and the stifled debate on national policies all meant that the process of decision-making was fraught with tension. At the present time, the dysfunctionality of this system of political decision-making has engendered pressures for a decompression and opening up of the system. Which trend proves to be uppermost will depend on the outcome of the political conflict.

In the second place, the marginalisation of the mass of the work force from the market produced tendencies towards economic stagnation and posed a serious problem of the eventual reincorporation of these people into the model. The level of unemployment and underemployment in Third World countries is phenomenally high, and the Brazilian model accentuates these problems.

Thirdly, the inflow of foreign capital was not an unmixed blessing. It is frequently assumed that the entry of foreign capital into an underdeveloped country constitutes an addition to the small stock of capital in existence and is therefore to be welcomed. This is a belief shared by some Marxists, who see this as a way in which imperialism will help to develop the Third World and so create the conditions of its own demise. This, at any rate, appears to have been the view of Marx himself. And the writings of Marxists such as Lenin clearly suggest a trend for capital to be exported from the advanced countries to the countries of the Third World. What seems to have been overlooked is that, to the extent that profits are transferred back to the imperialist metropolis, there will sooner or later be a return flow of profit. In time, the net return flow must exceed the net outflow, since otherwise the return on the capital invested overseas would be negative. Of course, the capitalist always has the option of reinvesting his profits locally, but this can only delay the time when profit outflow is likely to occur. In itself, the fact that the outflow will, in the long run, be greater than the inflow of capital might be quite acceptable. The long-term net outflow of capital might be seen as the cost of immediate injection of capital into the host economy, to be set off against the economic growth that occurred as a result of that injection of capital.

This argument is quite valid, though if it were possible actually to evaluate the costs and benefits involved, whether or not the contribution of foreign capital was negative or positive would still be an open matter. However, there is a dubious assumption underlying the argument. This assumption is that capital is in short supply in the economies of the Third World, and that the capital brought in by the foreign enterprise would not otherwise have been available for investment. There are a number of reasons for rejecting this assumption.

In the first place, a great deal of the capital which is under the control of the multinational enterprises is in fact raised locally. Rather than supplement local savings, foreign capital may simply be the form in which they are mobilised. Not only may its contribution be nil, as this argument suggests, it may even be negative if, instead of 'supplementing or channelling domestic savings, it actually supplants them (Griffin, 1971).

These arguments apply even if we consider capital as a disembodied resource. Once we admit that the end-product may not be appropriate for the underdeveloped country, then we have added yet another line of argument to suggest that foreign capital may have a negative impact on long-term development.

There is, then, no simple formula which will generate economic growth. Policy-makers in the Third World are faced with a large number of difficult and technically complex choices. But in the end, these boil down to a limited number of growth models. Each model is compatible with only a limited range of social and political structures. The choice of growth model is not a purely economic choice, made in a vacuum; it is made in a specific political and social context and entails specific social and political consequences.

Depending on the economic infrastructure, underdeveloped countries have a greater or lesser potential for autarchic development. Although autarchic development requires a long period of intensive capital accumulation during which living standards cannot rise very rapidly, it has the supreme advantage of giving the dominant class total control over the course of development.

If we define development as an increase in the capacity for controlled transformation of the social structure, then almost by definition, a move away from dependency to autarchy is a move in the direction of development. Whether this move is worthwhile depends on the cost of the economic growth (weighed against the cost of similar growth if the economy remained integrated into the world economy).

For a country such as China, such autarchic growth may prove to be the best choice. But for many Third World countries such a growth model is impossible simply because they lack the necessary resource base. These countries must continue to be integrated into the world capitalist economy or into the economic system of the socialist bloc. In either case, the first question must concern their exports.

Reliance on a single-commodity export is, above all, risky. In certain situations, the market position of the exporting nation may be favourable. This is clearly the case with the oil-exporting nations, and it has been the case with other commodities. But for most commodities, it is unwise to rely on a favourable market position in the long run. (How the revenues from exports are used, and whether they help a development programme, is a separate issue.) It makes sense, then, for many countries to (a) diversify exports and (b) attempt to export manufactured goods. But an export diversification programme involves certain costs, and if these new exports are competitive in terms of the allocation of productive resources with the principal export product, revenues from exports will drop during the initial phase of diversification. It may be that a government simply does not have the political strength to oversee this transitional period, and the attempt may have to be abandoned.

A similar difficulty concerns the relationship between manufacturing interests and export policy. (If there is a separate class of agrarian exporters and a separate class of industrial bourgeoisie, this policy conflict may be directly translatable into class terms. This will not, however, always be the case.) Manufacturers will generally want protectionist measures in order to reduce competition with foreign manufacturers. If this means an overvalued exchange rate, exporters of primary commodities may be put at a disadvantage and, given that the balance of payments is likely to be negative, there will be domestic inflation which will erode working-class support for the regime. The flow of foreign capital in and out of the country will also immediately be affected. For an underdeveloped country, decisions about exchange rates and the balance of payments will have almost immediate political repercussions. These kinds of economic decisions form the stuff of politics.

For example, if the ECLA argument about declining terms of trade is accepted, then there will be a persistent tendency towards balance of payments disequilibrium, so long as a fixed exchange rate is maintained. If this is accompanied, as the ECLA economists argued that it would be, by inflationary pressures stemming from market imperfections in the underdeveloped country itself, then governments will need to resort periodically to devaluation and orthodox price stabilisation measures. This will mean a cut in real wages. Where the organised working class or middle class is in a position to respond to such an attack on their standard of living by demonstrations and strikes, a situation of political instability is likely to emerge. The pressures will then build up for an authoritarian solution to the political situation, and the probability of a military *coup* will increase dramatically (Skidmore, 1977; Merkx, 1973).

Of course, there is nothing mechanical about this sequence of events; much will depend on the relative strengths of the various actors, on the power of those in control of the state, on divisions within the military, etc.

If a Third World country opts to continue to rely principally on one or two primary exports, and on foreign capital for technology, it must consider a series of measures to maximise its advantages and ensure that the economy is not too vulnerable to economic fluctuations. As the domestic bourgeoisie is usually quite weak, this will generally mean moves towards an increased role for the state in the running of the country. Such moves in the direction of statist developmentalism are bound to alter the balance of class forces and a frequent result will be the installation of some form of Bonapartist regime.

4

The World System

In recent years, this search for the internal obstacles to development, with its paradoxical (given its origins) neglect of imperialism, has come under increasing attack by the theorists of the new dependency school. Increasingly, analysts have been forced to focus on the fact that theories which assume that the processes of social change are endogenous to the societies of the Third World are completely ahistorical. Quite the reverse is true; change in the Third World is primarily the consequence of the externalisation of Western European capitalism through the formation of a world market and through various forms of imperialism and colonialism. One attempt to deal with this fact is embodied in the various theories of dependency, most of which spring from attempts to rethink the ECLA analysis in the light of the failure of its programmes of ISI to overcome underdevelopment.

The appearance of these theories is a relatively new phenomenon; as recently as 1969, writing about one part of the Third World, Oswaldo Sunkel could claim 'if one examines the writings of economists, sociologists and political scientists in Latin America, external dependence as a subject is remarkably absent' (Sunkel, 1969, p. 24). Even after making allowance for some exaggeration in Sunkel's claim, the rapid proliferation of works dealing with the issue of dependency or working within the framework of what is frequently (and loosely) referred to as 'dependency theory' is impressive.

The central insight of the dependency theorists was that it was of limited value to study the development of the societies of the Third World in isolation from the development of the advanced societies. From the point of view of dependency theories, it was necessary to treat the world as one single system. With this as the starting point, the problem was to discover the manner in which the underdeveloped countries were inserted into this world system, and how this differentiated them from the historical pattern of development of the advanced nations.

This insight was not, of course, entirely original. Marx, for one, had stressed the importance of the development of a world capitalist economic system as a force linking the fates of the developed and underdeveloped societies to each other (Marx, 1965, p. 49). Marx, as is well known, believed that the spread of capitalism over the globe would create in the underdeveloped countries the conditions which would result in a process of capital accumulation and economic growth basically similar to that occurring in the West. 'The country that is more developed industrially only shows to the less developed, the image of its own future' (Marx, 1909, p. xvii). As is equally well known, Marx was mistaken in this belief; the dynamic expansion of imperialism in the latter half of the nineteenth century did not result in the economic development of the colonies.

In one of the earliest articles to appear in the English language, dependency was defined as the obverse side of a theory of imperialism (Bodenheimer, 1970). If an analysis of the relations between developed and underdeveloped societies that focused on the processes occurring in the developed half of the equation produced a theory of imperialism, then if attention was systematically focused on the other half of the equation, the underdeveloped societies, a theory of dependency would be produced. In this sense, dependency theories would seek to explain the social and economic processes occurring in the 'imperialised' or dependent countries.

Implicit in this formulation of dependency as the other side of imperialism was the conclusion that, just as there were several, mutually inconsistent theories of imperialism, so there would also be several theories of dependency. The implications of this seem to have been only imperfectly grasped for several years, and it is possible to find references to 'the theory of dependency' as if there were only one. But, as has been argued above, the notion of dependency defines a paradigm rather than a specific theory. The failure to note that the term is used in a variety of ways has led to considerable confusion as scholars have argued 'for' or 'against' the use of a dependency perspective. Within the paradigm there are a number of competing theories and explanations of the nature of dependency.

These multiple uses of the term 'dependency' can be reduced to two basic approaches. On the one hand, a frequent approach has been to conceptualise dependency as some form of boundary interchange, as the dependence of one system on another. This may be labelled 'external' dependency, or 'dependency as a relationship'. On the other hand it is possible to view dependency as a conditioning factor which alters the internal functioning and articulation of the elements of the dependent social formation. The crucial distinction between the two approaches is that in the second approach the internal dynamics of the dependent social formation are fundamentally different from the internal dynamics of the social formations of advanced capitalism.

In its early formulations by ECLA economists, dependency was seen as a purely economic relationship between two national economies (or between two aggregated groups of national economies), in which the economic development of the dependent nations was conditioned by the economic development of the metropolitan nations. Dependency here came to mean 'lack of autonomy'. Various mechanisms whereby this relationship of dependency came into being and was sustained were suggested. Prominent among them was the postulated long-term tendency for the terms of trade to move in favour of the industrialised nations.

But by treating the phenomenon of dependency as a relation between 'economies', the term 'dependency' came to mean no more than non-autonomous. As P. O'Brien has pointed out in a perceptive article, this has a tendency to result in a circular argument: 'dependent countries are those which lack the capacity for autonomous growth and they lack this because their structures are dependent ones' (O'Brien, 1975, p. 24). Clearly, the central issue – the nature of these dependent structures and the differences between them and the structures of advanced societies – remained unsolved. What in effect the ECLA economists ·had done was to jump over the intervening level of social structure. They had ignored the specific class interests and the relationships between classes which led to the continual reproduction of the structures of dependency.

An early and influential attempt to deal with this problem was made by Frank. He utilised the metaphor of a chain of exploitative relations; an extraction and transmission of surplus through a series of metropolis–satellite links. While on a global scale one could visualise the relationship between the countries of the industrialised West and the non-industrialised Third World as a relationship between metropolis and satellite, this metropolis–satellite tie also characterised the relationship within the underdeveloped country between the (relatively) advanced capital city and the (even more) oppressed and backward hinterland. Nor was this chain confined merely to spatial regions. One of the distinctive characteristics of Frank's social theory has been the conflation of spatial entities and social classes (Booth, 1975, p. 78), so that the relationship between landowner and peasant is also characterised as a form of metropolis–satellite tie *exactly comparable* to the links between spatial regions.

It is this conflation, and the use of a concept of surplus to replace the Marxist concept of surplus-value, which enables Frank to encompass two apparently disparate phenomena (relations of exploitation among social classes and relations of transfer of value between economic regions) with the simple metaphor of a series of metropolis–satellite links stretching from the Bolivian peasant in an unbroken chain to the rich New York capitalist (O'Brien, 1975, p. 27). This imagery is perhaps most graphically expressed by Jonathan Swift:

> So, naturalists observe, a flea
> Hath smaller fleas that on him prey;
> And these have smaller fleas to bite 'em,
> And so proceed *ad infinitum*.

It should perhaps be stressed that we are not criticising Frank for neglecting to analyse the class structure (though some commentators might think this would also be an appropriate comment) but for the way in which he integrates classes into his analysis. In his first major work, Frank stated:

> The attempt to spell out the metropolis–satellite colonial structure and development of capitalism has led me to devote very little specific attention to its class structure and development. This does not mean that this colonial analysis is intended as a substitute for class analysis. On the contrary, the colonial analysis is meant to complement class analysis and to discover and empha-

sise aspects of the class structure in these underdeveloped countries which have often remained unclear. (Frank, 1967, p. xi)

Unfortunately, intentions are not always translated into accomplishments. One of the criticisms made of Frank's work was precisely that he did *not* analyse the relations of exploitation in terms of social classes (Frank, 1972, p. 1). Frank's reply was emphatically to reaffirm the importance of understanding underdevelopment in terms of classes (Frank, 1972, p. 1). The important point is not that Frank neglects class analysis, but rather the manner in which he undertakes it. While Frank's analysis of colonialism purports to rest on class relations of capitalist exploitation, it in fact treats such relations as residual. That is to say, the conceptualisation of class relations, which is present in the theory, is accorded little or no role in the analysis of relations of domination and exploitation, which are instead conceived of as occurring between spatial categories.

On the contrary, flows of value between spatial regions can only be adequately accounted for in terms of the distribution and redistribution of surplus-value (together with value produced as a result of primitive accumulation) among social classes. This distribution does not necessarily directly reflect the production of surplus-value through the exploitation of labour-power. That is to say, the transfer of value from one region to another is not necessarily the same phenomenon as the direct exploitation of labour-power. This transfer may be analysed in terms of unequal exchange, or as a question of the redistribution of surplus-value amongst the non-productive classes, or in terms of non-correspondence between class structure and economic regions.

This latter situation might arise if the capitalist class in an underdeveloped country were, for example, entirely foreign and simply invested the surplus-value extracted in the underdeveloped country in the developed country, thereby creating a net outflow of capital and producing a process of capital accumulation which, looked at from the point of view of the underdeveloped country and treating that economy as a unit, would be entirely different from that which Marx thought would occur under capitalism. While the system as a whole might continue to operate according to the laws of motion of capitalism, each of its component parts (the developed half and the underdeveloped half) would exhibit different patterns of growth.

There would in this case be a real non-correspondence between class structure and the political framework of the nation-state since, while there would only be *one* capitalist class there would be (at least) two subordinate classes (one in each country). To deny the reality of this problem by appeals to the international solidarity of the world working class is to confuse actuality with potentiality. Since classes are generally formed on the national level (Bettelheim, 1972, p. 301; Genovese, 1971, p. 21; Thompson, 1963, p. 11), the concepts of class struggle and exploitation only have meaning at the level of the social formation. To say, as Amin does, that:

> . . . capitalism has become a world system, and not just a juxtaposition of 'national capitalisms'. The social contradictions characteristic of capitalism are thus on a world scale, that is, the contradiction is not between the bourgeoisie and the proletariat of each country considered in isolation, but between the world bourgeoisie and the world proletariat. (Amin, 1974, p. 24)

is to slide from the level of analysis appropriate to the economic system of capitalism (worldwide) to that appropriate to social formations (generally national).

These theoretical problems are not without their consequences for the analysis of classes. This is *prima facie* surprising, for one of the initial concerns of Frank's work was the correct formation of class alliances in order to bring about a socialist revolution in Latin America. We shall return to the question of the class structure in Chapter 6.

What is perhaps the most devastating critique of Frank's work has been made by Ernesto Laclau (Laclau, 1971). Starting from Frank's claim that Latin America has been a capitalist society since the beginning of the sixteenth century, Laclau argues that Frank's definition of capitalism differs radically from the Marxist one, since it emphasises exchange and commercial relationships rather than the processes of production. In particular, Frank confuses participation in the world capitalist economic system with the dominance of the capitalist mode of production in Latin America. The manner in which the key terms of capitalism and feudalism are defined determines the entire methodology employed and the conclusions (and political practice) deduced from the theory.

The debate between Frank and Laclau repeats in many ways a previous debate carried on in the pages of *Science and Society* over the transition from feudalism to capitalism in Western Europe (Hilton *et al.*, 1976). In that debate, a number of theorists put forward the view that the defining characteristics of feudalism were the absence of large-scale commerce, the self-sufficiency of the manor and production for use rather than for exchange. As Sternberg has noted (Sternberg, 1974, p. 77), this view springs directly from Pirenne's work and has affinities with Weber's methodology. Following this line of reasoning, it is sufficient to demonstrate the dominant role of production for the market to show that the society in question is not feudal but capitalist. This is precisely the position taken by Frank. As Brenner has argued, this concern for the market has its origins in Adam Smith's classic work, *The Wealth of Nations* (Brenner, 1977).

The evidence Frank employs to demonstrate that the economies of Latin America produced primarily for the market, and were from the very beginning of the Conquest tied closely to the nascent world market, is not here in question. Frank's marshalling of the data is not at issue (though, clearly, some historical researchers may seriously dispute his presentation of 'the facts'). What are at issue are the conclusions drawn from that data. To conclude, as Frank does, that Latin America was capitalist from the time of the Conquest on, produces a number of theoretical problems, which have not gone unnoticed.

Not least among these problems is the implication that if the Iberians implanted a capitalist society in the New World in the early sixteenth century, then Spain and Portugal must have been capitalist societies at that time. It is not likely that this argument would be widely accepted. Moreover, to 'argue that capitalism – even of a dependent variety – gained predominance in satellite areas of Latin America before it gained predominance in England or Spain certainly appears inconsistent with Marx's historical analysis of the times' (Sternberg, 1974, p. 78).

Frank attempts to overcome this difficulty by arguing that it was the mercantile capitalist *sector* of Iberian society which was responsible for the implantation of capitalism in Latin America. This simply pushes the same problems back one stage further.

Frank's theses . . . obscure the nature of class rule and present

us with two insoluble problems, the first being the impossibility
of locating the process by which the bourgeoisie assumed state
power in Spain and Portugal, and the second, the impossibility
of accounting for the acquiescence of a seigneurial state in an
economic process sponsored by and primarily benefiting the bourgeoisie. (Genovese, 1969, p. 61.)

If Frank were claiming that he was a Marxist, these would
all be telling criticisms of his methodology. It is not the production
of commodities as such which defines the capitalist mode of production for Marxists, but rather the existence of labour-power as a
commodity, and it is not the absence of markets but the existence
of servile labour which defines feudalism as a mode of production.

However, Frank has never claimed to be a Marxist (Frank,
1974, p. 96). It might seem, therefore, that this lengthy exercise
to demonstrate that Frank is not a Marxist is redundant. Perhaps.
But Frank nowhere says that he is *not* a Marxist, and his critics
continue to treat him as one. If it were merely a question of
attaching labels, of making sure that all theorists were neatly classified and pigeon-holed for future reference, it would be trivial
to pursue this matter. Our justification is that there has been
considerable theoretical confusion because of the lack of precision
in distinguishing radically different methodologies, based on radically different notions of capitalism and feudalism.

Implicit in all the theories which we have examined so far
have been sets of assumptions about the unit of analysis. While
this may seem an extremely abstract issue, it is of tremendous
consequence for the kind of explanation of underdevelopment which
is eventually adopted. The everyday notion that the units of analysis
are nation-states or national societies needs to be considered critically. For the societies of the Third World, there are two considerations; the recently-formed nations which comprise the Third
World are by no means well-integrated and homogenous entities.
Regional differences, ethnic and linguistic cleavages, and the simple
absence of any sense of nationhood among many of the rural
inhabitants are one dimension of this lack of internal articulation.
Another dimension is the difficulty which the central state actually
has in implementing policies in the peripheral parts of its territory.
The second consideration is the complement of the first. Just as
these societies are badly articulated internally, some parts of them

are closely integrated with the metropoli of advanced capitalism. The classic case is an export enclave, in which the mineral-producing region or the region of export-oriented agriculture is closely tied to the external market, and is frequently foreign owned, but is only connected to the local economy via the tax revenues that the host government can get from it. The Chilean nitrate and copper industries provide a good example of this kind of export enclave.

However, so important is this dual internal-disarticulation external-articulation phenomenon that some analysts focus on this in their definition of dependency. Girvan has noted that the 'necessary corollary of such external dependence is a lack of internal structural interdependence between many of the most important elements of the economic system' (Girvan, 1973, p. 11), and he quotes Brewster as saying:

> Economic dependence may be defined as a lack of capacity to manipulate the operative elements of an economic system. Such a situation is characterised by an absence of inter-dependence between the economic functions of a system. This lack of inter-dependence implies that the system has no internal dynamic which would enable it to function as independent, autonomous entity. (Cited Girvan, 1973, p. 11)

There are two aspects of this articulation of the dependent economy with the world capitalist economic system. *Within* the social formation of the dependent country there is the articulation of the modes of production in the interior of the historically given social formation. At the level of its interconnections with the world economy, there is the articulation between the dependent economy and other economies. The two aspects are interrelated. The manner in which the economy is inserted into the world economy conditions the processes of articulation of modes of production within the social formation of the dependent country.

This interaction of 'internal' and 'external' is, as was pointed out, the central question in theories of dependency. The 'internal'/ 'external' question has been highlighted by Quartim. He notes:

> The sense which can be assigned to the concept of dependency is that of a knowledge of a specific object which is itself a

partial system (a sub-system) of a larger system (the international capitalist system) which determines it in the last instance, without determining it completely ... It is necessary to conceive of it as the complex unity of a double process of the historical development of capitalism on the international scale and of each one of the dependent societies, and hence as a synthesis of 'external factors' and 'internal factors'. (Quartim, 1972, pp. 16–17)

However, one must go beyond the simple recognition of internal and external factors by posing

the question of the genesis of dependency as a specific form of domination ... determined in the first instance by the class struggle and the development of capitalism in the interior of the economic formations of the dependent societies and in the last instance by the periods of the development of capitalism on a world scale. (Quartim, 1972, p. 17)

The question of the exact nature of the interconnection between 'internal' and 'external' factors is a real question, for which no easy answer is forthcoming. Quartim's own attempted resolution of the problem is the classic appeal to the determination of the last instance, an old Althusserian bug-bear. This formulation seems to raise as many problems as it appears to solve. Like the flight of Minerva's owl, the coming of the last instance remains a remarkably elusive event of dubious epistemological status and utility.
A radical way of dealing with the external–internal problem has been suggested by Wallerstein. He abolishes the distinction altogether by making the world system his unit of analysis. He says that he

abandoned the idea altogether of taking either the sovereign state or that vaguer concept, the national society, as the unit of analysis. I decided that neither one was a social system and that one could only speak of social change in social systems. The only social system in this scheme was the world system. (Wallerstein, 1974, p. 7)

This is similar to the position put forward by Frank and other writers such as Sunkel who are in the ECLA tradition. However, the notion of a world system forms the focus of Wallerstein's work in a way that it does not in the work of the dependency theorists, where it serves the primary function of defining a set of external influences which explain the underdevelopment of the Third World.

Like Frank's analysis, Wallerstein's understanding of the nature of the world system implies a shift in the concept of mode of production. His conclusion is the same as Frank's (that is, that all the component parts of the world system are equally to be characterised as capitalist). He argues that

> the relations of production that define a system are the relations of production of the whole system, and the system at this point in time is the European world economy. Free labor is indeed a defining feature of capitalism, but not free labor throughout the productive enterprises. Free labor is the form of labor control used for skilled work in core countries whereas coerced labor is used for less skilled work in peripheral areas. The combination thereof is the essence of capitalism. (Wallerstein, 1974, p. 127)

The differences with Frank are not great, and Wallerstein too is open to Laclau's point that participation in a world economy is not a sufficient reason to define something as capitalist.

Wallerstein, of course, is absolutely correct in his emphasis on the way in which the expansion of Western European capitalism overseas *created* forms of coerced labour which had either not been known in the West or had been superseded. As Eric Williams and Genovese have shown in detail, the class of landowners in the slave societies of the Americas was intimately linked to the capitalist societies of Europe, even though it did, however, comprise a distinct class or class fraction. There is no easy resolution of the question of the unit of analysis, if only because the real world is neither a perfectly integrated system nor a loose collection of autonomously functioning national societies. The boundaries are drawn, it may be suggested, by the historical formation of social classes. What the boundaries of any given unit of analysis are, is therefore an historical question and cannot be settled beforehand by theoretical deliberation except in the most abstract way.

The manner in which the periphery and the centre are linked together is a function of the development of the centre itself. At different stages in its historical evolution the centre will be articulated with the countries of the periphery in different ways. (We return to this in the discussion of theories of imperialism in the next chapter.) Therefore, a first step in any analysis must be a periodisation of the stages of development of the centre. Only then can a typology of Third World countries be added to the schema.

Osvaldo Sunkel has suggested such a periodisation for Latin America (Sunkel and Paz, 1970). A simplified version might be as shown in Table 1.

TABLE I   *Historical development of centre and periphery*

	Centre	*World power*	*Latin America*
1850–1930	Mature capitalism	GB	Export economies; liberal trade regimes
1930–50	Crisis	USA	ISI
1960–	Late monopoly capitalism; MNCs	USA	Dependent authoritarian capitalism; neo-liberal trade regimes

SOURCE   Adapted from Sunkel and Paz (1970).

The way in which different countries within Latin America, and countries in different continents of the underdeveloped world were integrated into the world economy at different times will obviously vary to a considerable extent, and a fuller version of Table 1 would be extremely complex.

Once seen in these terms, the sociology of development begins to look rather like a version of world history. If this were the case, then the theory-formulation aspect of sociology would drop out of the picture and we would be left with an idiographic account of a single and unique occurrence. To a certain extent this is true, but in so far as we take our unit of analysis to be the nation-states of the Third World, since it can reasonably be argued that at the present time these are in fact the arenas in which social classes are formed and fight out their conflicts, we do have a number of more or less similar phenomena which we can generalise about and form sociological theories of.

However, we cannot simply assume that all underdeveloped societies are basically similar and immediately proceed to make generalising statements about them. Before we do this an analysis of modes of insertion into the world capitalist economy and a study of the formation of social classes is necessary in order that like be compared with like.

5
Imperialism and Dependency

Originally, theories of imperialism sought to explain the absence of a profound economic crisis in the capitalist nations of Western Europe. They attempted to account for the continued growth of capitalism by focusing on the way in which the acquisition of colonies had enabled European powers to export capital and thereby postpone crises at home. Thus, the interest of these theorists of imperialism lay in the *causes* of imperialism in the metropolitan nations, rather than in its *effects* on the economic growth of the rest of the world.

Two of the earliest theories of imperialism are those of Hobson and Lenin. There are so many similarities that the two theories have sometimes been treated as identical, as the 'Hobson–Lenin thesis'.

Hobson argued that there was insufficient effective demand in the metropolis, owing to low wages, and that consequently, capitalists needed to find markets for their commodities overseas. He believed that income redistribution would remedy this problem of underconsumption (Kemp, 1967). Lenin's argument was rather different. He argued that the declining rate of profit in the metropolis meant that, with the opening up of the colonies, there were more profitable investment opportunities abroad. Lenin claimed that imperialism was characterised by a net outflow of capital to the colonies (Lenin, 1966).

The implication of both Hobson's and Lenin's theories, as well as the earlier comments by Marx (Avineri, 1969), was that, whether the mechanism was a push from the metropolis or a pull from the periphery, there would, in the long run, be capital accumulation in the periphery and an eventual equalisation of rates of profit between metropolis and periphery. The failure of this equalisation to occur produced substantial modifications of the Leninist theory of imperialism, which I will examine shortly.

One important feature of Lenin's treatment of imperialism must be singled out. Lenin did not conceive of imperialism as a relationship between two states or between two economies. Rather, he saw it as a stage in the development of capitalism. Imperialism, then, was the label attached to a stage in the development of capitalism characterised by five features: (1) the dominance of monopolies; (2) the dominance of finance capital; (3) the export of capital (rather than the export of commodities); (4) the formation of international monopolies; (5) the partition of the world between the various imperialist powers. These five features may be summarised as monopolisation plus colonies. Implicit in this definition of imperialism as a phase of capitalism is an assertion of a necessary connection between colonies and monopoly capital. The definition and the theory are one and the same. If one is rejected, the other must be, too.

Lenin claimed that imperialism was the highest stage of capitalism. That proposition can no longer be sustained. The post-war epoch has witnessed a process of decolonisation without the collapse of monopoly capital. If Lenin's description was accurate for the early twentieth century (and there may be serious doubts about that) it certainly does not apply now. We live in a different phase of capitalist development today. Whether we label this stage as 'late capitalism' (Mandel, 1975) or as the 'permanent arms economy' (Kidron, 1968), or something else, the basic point remains the same: there have been profound structural changes in capitalism since Lenin's time which suggest that his description of imperialism is not likely to prove particularly useful today. This is not merely a semantic point. If imperialism is defined as an inherent component of a stage of capitalist development, then the transcendence of that stage must call in question previously accepted notions of imperialism.

However, even as a description of the operation of the world economy at the turn of the century, Lenin's analysis is questionable. In the first place, the timing of the scramble for colonies and the development of the monopoly sector does not generally support Lenin's thesis. Clearly, other factors were also at work in the process of colonisation. In the second place, most of the capital exports went to a limited group of colonies – the colonies of white settlement (Australia, New Zealand, South Africa) rather than to the newly acquired possessions in East and West Africa. Thirdly, in the long run, the net flow of capital was inwards, towards the metropolis. Capital exports to the periphery have declined; most trade is *within* the metropolitan area. The countries of the periphery are exactly that – peripheral.

Whether one accepts these empirical arguments or not, Lenin's analysis of imperialism is open to a serious methodological criticism. When most people talk about imperialism they refer to some kind of relationship between countries or economies. This (and not a definition of imperialism as a stage in the development of capitalism) seems to be the only useful way of proceeding.

James O'Connor has defined imperialism as the 'formal or informal control over local economic resources in a manner advantageous to the metropolitan power, and at the expense of the local economy' (O'Connor, 1970a, p. 118). If, for the moment, we take this as a working definition, it will be clear that this relationship may assume many forms and the *mechanisms* of imperialism may be multiple. Also, the definition does not formally associate imperialism only with capitalism. It is formally possible for imperialist relations to exist in non-capitalist systems. It seems unreasonable not to label many of the ancient empires (Rome, China, etc.) 'imperialist'. Clearly they fit the definition. One might wish to argue that the imperialism of the ancient empires and the imperialism of contemporary capitalism are quite different phenomena. Perhaps so. So also were the wars of ancient empires and of modern capitalism – but we would still say that they were all wars nevertheless.

Using a formal definition of imperialism, such as O'Connor's, requires us to specify the *content* of the imperialist relation, how it works, and in what circumstances it will operate. Most theories of imperialism have insisted on the existence of one particular mechanism of imperialism, one particular form of imperialist relationship. This seems a trifle premature. The alternative possibility, that *various* mechanisms of imperialism operate, simultaneously or in different historical phases, or between different types of economy, seems quite plausible. Consequently, one of the arguments against some theories of imperialism may be that they are incomplete and restricted, rather than absolutely incorrect.

For example, Harry Magdoff argues that the principal reason
for the pull of capital abroad lies in the need for metropolitan
capital to control certain sources of scarce raw materials (Magdoff,
1969). There may well be some truth in this argument (though,
as Szymanski has argued, even in its own terms Magdoff's argument
may be greatly exaggerated), but it can hardly account for all
forms of imperialist penetration in the Third World (Szymanski,
1977).

Some theories of imperialism are incompatible with others, but
this is not universally the case. For example, the set of theories
concerned with the effects of unequal exchange are, in general,
quite compatible with theories which stress the deleterious effects
of foreign investment.

The early theorists of imperialism paid little attention to the
effects of foreign capital investment in the underdeveloped countries,
generally assuming that such effects were benign. There are reasons
to view this assumption critically. The data reveal a net *outflow*
of capital from the Third World to the metropolis. That is, for
every dollar invested in the Third World, more than one dollar
returns to the metropolis in the form of repatriated profits, royalties,
services, repayment of debt and interest, etc. The official data
on the flow of capital almost certainly underestimate the magnitude
of the flow (Müller, 1973). The net effect of foreign investment
is to create an outflow of capital from the periphery to the metropolis. (The effect this has on the economic functioning of the
metropolis is beyond the scope of this book. Briefly, it seems that
the problem of overaccumulation has been 'solved' by a variety
of mechanisms for the absorption of surplus in the form of waste.
This has taken its most noticeable form in the development of
a permanent arms economy (Kidron, 1968).)

Even though the net flow of capital is outward from the Third
World, it could still be argued that the net contribution of foreign
capital to economic growth was positive. This would be the case
if the increment in GNP produced by foreign investment (taking
into account multiplier and accelerator effects) was greater than
the net capital outflow. In this case, the net capital outflow would
be the cost of obtaining the increment of economic growth.

The logic of the argument is perfectly acceptable. But its validity
depends on a set of *ceteris paribus* assumptions about the use to
which economic resources would have been put in the absence

of foreign investment. The general assumption behind the argument for foreign capital is that in its absence, little or none of the increment in growth which it engendered would be produced by local resources as these are either fully employed elsewhere or non-existent. Such an assumption does not apply to many under-developed countries.

Keith Griffin has argued that foreign capital, rather than supplement domestic savings, actually substitutes for them. He claims that this is true both for private capital investment and for various forms of foreign aid (Griffin, 1971). A large percentage of capital under foreign control is, in fact, raised locally. It is more rational for domestic portfolio investors to put their money into multinational corporations, which have immense resources and technological capability, than into smaller, domestic enterprises which are more likely to have lower profit rates and higher risks. Banking and financial institutions are more likely to advance credit to multinational corporations (MNCs) than to local enterprises (Barnett and Müller, 1974).

The consequence is that local capital increasingly comes under the control of the MNCs in the modern, dynamic sectors of the economy, while the more backward sectors of the economy are left to local capital. Only massive state intervention is likely to alter this process. Of course, if the profits accruing to foreign capital are reinvested locally, this merely postpones the date of eventual capital outflow while simultaneously increasing the share of domestic industry controlled by foreign capital (since its profit rates and growth rates are usually higher than those of local capital).

In general, therefore, the presumption that the investment of foreign capital serves to transfer real resources from periphery to metropolis seems a plausible one. To repeat, this does not necessarily mean that foreign capital does not make a positive contribution to economic growth, only that the transfer of real resources is higher than it would have been if somehow domestic capital had been used instead of foreign capital. It is here that one of the most forcible arguments for state intervention may be found. Only the state, in the countries of the Third World, can organise the resources necessary for massive investment projects, and only the state can break away from a narrow and short-term concern with profitability.

But although the state may be able to organise the capital

necessary for such ventures, it may not have access to the appropriate technology. With very minor qualifications, it can be said that the MNCs and the developed nations have a monopoly of modern technology. To obtain access to this technology, the Third World must pay for it. The Third World simply does not have the capacity to create its own scientific establishment capable of making technological innovations competitive with those of the centre.

However, the technology produced by advanced capitalism is principally capital-intensive and labour-saving. Given the resource endowments of the Third World, it is questionable whether the technology produced by the advanced nations is suitable for the underdeveloped countries. But if the Third World countries are to operate on the world market, they have little option but to use modern technology since, on a world scale, this is the only competitive way to produce. In the absence of some form of intermediate technology appropriate to their own special circumstances, underdeveloped countries are forced to pay heavily for technology which displaces already overabundant labour.

Whether the payments for this technology should be included as a form of imperialism is a moot point. The monopoly of technology certainly operates to the advantage of the metropolis and to the disadvantage of the periphery, and doubtless monopoly profits are obtained. Whether this counts as imperialism or not must surely depend on whether the price paid for the technology approximates its cost plus normal profit, that is, on whether there exists some form of equal exchange.

The notion of the equal exchange of commodities is central to Marxist economics. In *Capital*, Marx presupposes the equal exchange of equivalents, that is, a commodity embodying X hours of socially-necessary labour-time will exchange with another commodity embodying the same amount of socially-necessary labour-time. The two critical assumptions are: (1) that the value of commodities can be measured in terms of the average number of average man-hours needed to produce it, with a given level of technology; and (2) that the economic system is competitive and in long-run equilibrium so that there is a free movement of the factors of production (otherwise there would be no meaning to the notion of 'socially-necessary labour-time').

If we accept the first assumption but not the second, then we have the conditions for unequal exchange. There are a number of different theories of unequal exchange. What they have in common is a proposition that labour is rewarded unequally in different parts of the world and hence identical commodities may embody different amounts of socially-necessary labour-time. When one commodity is exchanged for another, behind the transaction is an exchange of a greater quantum of socially-necessary labour-time for a lesser. The exchange is unequal and works to the disadvantage of the underdeveloped countries. The same amount of labour-time may be embodied in each commodity, but the remuneration of that labour is different. If the value of labour-time is the cost of its reproduction, that is, a certain basket of goods at any determinate historical epoch, then more value goes into the commodity produced in the metropolis (real wages are higher) than into the identical commodity produced in the periphery. So that a commodity which embodies X days labour is exchanged against an identical commodity produced in the Third World which embodies more than X days labour. A greater quantity of labour is exchanged for a lesser, assuming that technology and labour productivity are held constant. This is the essence of unequal exchange. Because labour is rewarded unequally, the exchange of commodities carries with it an unequal exchange of labour, and hence, of value.

Some critics have argued against the theory of unequal exchange, pointing out that, according to the theory, exploitation takes place in the sphere of circulation and not in the sphere of production. This is hardly a satisfactory criticism. If exploitation occurs in the sphere of circulation rather than of production, this does not invalidate the theory of unequal exchange so much as invalidate those crude versions of Marxism which insist that only the sphere of production is 'real' and that circulation is only an epiphenomenon.

There is, however, a more interesting comment to be made about unequal exchange. If the second assumption on which Marx's economic theories were built is not accepted, then it is no longer possible to continue to hold the first assumption. Once it is accepted that equal amounts of equally productive and equally skilled labour, with identical technology, are rewarded unequally (that is, that real wage rates differ from one country to the next), then it is no longer possible to assume that the measure of value – socially-necessary labour-time – has any unique value.

Marx's assumption was that, at any given historical period, the notion of a single value for average wages was a meaningful one. This was to be the measure of value. Once it is accepted that real wage rates differ greatly on the international scale, this assumption is untenable. Hence one cannot talk about a single world economic system to which unitary measures of value can be attached. If this is not possible, then the entire corpus of Marxist economics is inapplicable to the international economy. Thus, it would seem that a theory of unequal exchange and a labour theory of value are incompatible. Theories of unequal exchange, however, may be compatible with other theories of value.

The implication of theories of unequal exchange seems to be that exploitation may take place in the sphere of circulation, as well as in the sphere of production. If this is so, then the high wages of workers in advanced countries are, in part, a result of the low wages of workers in the periphery. Clearly this has serious implications for any discussion of the interests of the working classes in advanced and in peripheral countries (Emmanuel, 1972; Amin, 1974; Amin, 1976).

These arguments about unequal exchange tend to focus on the unequal rewards of labour, even if technology and labour productivity are held constant, and should therefore be clearly separated from arguments about inappropriate factor mixes.

Of course, as Kidron has pointed out, labour productivity and technology does differ, and this will reduce, though not eliminate, the extent of inequality in the exchange (Kidron, 1974).

What is the connection between imperialism and dependency? There may not be imperialism – in the sense that the metropolis does not derive any advantage from the relationship – but the underdeveloped economy may still suffer from the relationship. If imperialism focuses on the gains to the metropolis, dependency focuses on the disadvantages to the satellite. However, the term 'dependency' is ambiguous and has come to have several meanings. Let us examine the genesis of dependency theories, beginning with the failure of theories of imperialism to explain the continued economic stagnation of the Third World.

The question of why this should be so, why the expansion of capital overseas did nothing to generate economic growth in the colonies and ex-colonies, was relegated to a position of marginal importance beside the questions that taxed socialists in the advanced capitalist nations: what were the motivating forces of modern imperialism, and did it offer a solution to the crisis of capitalism? It is understandable that the impact of imperialism on the countries of the capitalist centre should have been the focus of debate; just as it is understandable that serious discussion of the problems of economic development in the periphery would be postponed until the period of the rapid dissolution of empire in the post-war world.

This long neglect resulted in serious theoretical gaps when, under the impact of dramatic political upsurges in the Third World, Western theorists began to turn their attention to developments in the former colonies. There existed hardly any serious and coherent theory which accounted for the effects of imperialism on the social structures and patterns of economic development of the countries of the Third World. The dominant theories at the time were the non-Marxist stages of growth and diffusionist theories, and the rather mechanical position adopted by the Communist parties: a position that generally advocated an alliance of the working class and peasantry with the 'progressive national bourgeoisie' against feudal or semi-feudal oligarchies and comprador bourgeoisies allied to imperialism.

It was in polemics with these theories that the paradigm of dependency was developed. The argument proceeded as follows: the mode of articulation of the underdeveloped economies with the world economic system may result in a transfer of resources from the periphery to the centre and/or this articulation may give rise to various 'blocking mechanisms' which hold back or 'distort' the economies of the periphery, thereby preventing an allocation of resources which will produce economic growth.

The transfer of value (resources) and the 'blocking' and 'distorting' effects can operate independently of each other, though in concrete cases they are likely to be interrelated in complex ways. Furthermore, the mechanisms by which value is transferred from periphery to centre are manifold. Value may be transferred by direct plunder, through unequal exchange, through the exchange of productive goods for non-productive goods, via a monopoly of shipping fleets, through control over prices, etc. The same holds for the mechanisms that produce blocking and distortion. They also are many and varied. Which of these mechanisms actually occur in a given case or in a given epoch is the subject of considerable debate.

It is possible for some of these mechanisms of imperialism (meaning here both the transfer of value and the blocking effects) to
occur between two capitalist countries (or to be more precise,
between two social formations in which the capitalist mode of
production is either exclusive or dominant). If this occurred (for
example, a flow of capital from Britain to the United States resulting
from American investment in Britain), although we might characterise one of these social formations as 'backward' or 'dependent'
(the British), we would not attempt to claim that the mode of
production or the social formation (the complex articulation of
modes of production) was in any radical way different from that
in the United States. In this sense it is possible, as Poulantzas
has argued, for relations of dependency to exist between metropolitan powers. However, this dependency is of a different nature
from that which characterises the relationships between the centre
and the periphery since the dependent but advanced metropolitan
nations continue to be independent centres of capital accumulation
(Poulantzas, 1974, p. 151).

If, then, the underdeveloped countries do not function in the
world economy in the same way as do the metropolitan powers
we are justified in treating Third World dependency as a distinct
phenomenon, not identical in nature to any relationships of dependency which may exist between advanced capitalist countries. We
might say, then, that there can be transfers of value between
two distinct modes of production.

The most consistent treatment of this is Marx's discussion of
the original or primitive accumulation (Marx, 1909; Marx, 1962).
Within a given social formation this may take the form of a transfer
of value from the feudal agricultural sector to the capitalist sector.
Between social formations, this takes the form of plunder and
primitive forms of colonialism.

Rosa Luxemburg's analysis suggested that this transfer of value
between modes of production was the central element in imperialism. (Luxemburg, 1951). According to her, twentieth-century imperialism involved primarily the expansion of the capitalist mode
of production into pre-capitalist modes of production. The dynamic
behind this process was an attempt to avert a realisation crisis
by finding a 'leak' in the capitalist economic system. This leak
was found by exchanging commodities at the boundary of the

system with other modes of production. (It should be noted that the role of the interaction between capitalist and pre-capitalist modes of production for the social formations of metropolitan capitalism changes from one historical epoch to another. When metropolitan capitalism is just coming into existence there is primitive accumulation of capital; as metropolitan capitalism matures the pre-capitalist formations of the periphery become a dumping ground for surplus-value which cannot be realised.) This notion of exchange between two modes of production is central to some of the theories of dependency, in particular those that claim that a central mechanism of imperialism consists in unequal exchange.

While most theories of dependency asserted that the dominant mode of production in the dependent social formation is capitalism, they point out either that this is a specific *kind* of capitalism, or that the social formations are different because they contain within them other modes of production (by keeping wages low, for example).

It is not clear what is implied in the claim that there is a specific kind of capitalism in the peripheral countries. Is it the case that peripheral dependent capitalism is a mode of production *sui generis*, with its own laws of motion? If not, why does it apparently not obey the laws of motion of capitalism (particularly capital accumulation)? These problems are simply pushed back one stage further if one asserts that the social formations of the periphery are complex totalities in which the operation of the capitalist mode of production is affected by the coexistence of other modes of production. For although one can account for the primitive accumulation of capital between the capitalist and pre-capitalist sectors within the interior of the dependent social formation, one is still left with the question of why and how that capital does not produce internal capitalist growth.

In the previous chapter, two distinct notions of dependency were noted: dependency as a relationship, and dependency as a set of structures. If dependency is viewed merely as a relationship between two countries then, as Quijano says,

the concept would have no other function than to replace, for certain purposes, the concept of 'imperialism', without providing the necessary understanding of how the articulation of elements produced by imperialist domination, giving rise to a determinate socio-economic formation subordinated to it, is carried out. (Quijano, 1974, pp. 398–9)

This distinction has been recognised by a number of theorists, including dos Santos, who defines dependency as:

a situation in which a certain group of countries have their economies conditioned by the development and expansion of another economy, to which their own is subjected. (Dos Santos, 1970b, p. 45)

Dependency conditions a certain internal structure which redefines it as a function of the structural possibilities of the distinct national economies. (Dos Santos, 1970b, p. 48)

It is this different economic structure which sets off dependent countries from the advanced countries and from the 'dependent advanced countries'.

Dos Santos' definition contains two parts. The first, which asserts that dependency is a relationship between two groups of economies (those that condition others and those that are conditioned by them) does not constitute an advance on previous formulations of the problem. After all, all economies are interdependent and condition each other reciprocally. Indeed, the basis of Magdoff's theory of imperialism is that the United States is dependent on Third World countries for supplies of essential raw materials (Magdoff, 1969). It appears that these formulations in terms of degrees of dependency and autonomy are not particularly helpful; the nature of the dependency must be specified. The second half of dos Santos' definition attempts to do just this: dependency is a certain internal structure different from that of the advanced nations.

It is when we attempt to conceptualise these differences in structure that difficulties occur. There seem to be two basic choices: either there is a mode of production in dependent countries which is different from that of capitalism; or, while the dependent countries have a capitalist mode of production, the articulation of the capitalist mode of production with the other modes of production in the social formation and with the economies of the advanced countries results in a different manner of functioning of that mode of production.

In terms of purely economic processes, this latter alternative presents few problems. As mentioned previously, Girvan's analysis of the input–output matrix of dependent economies presents a fruitful starting point.

We have tried to illustrate the difficulties arising from attempts to treat the social formations of the Third World as though they were basically similar to those of the advanced West. These differences result in a different functioning of the economy in the under-developed societies. We have argued that these differences cannot be accounted for merely by treating dependency as a relationship (external dependency), but have to be analysed by treating dependency as a set of structures.

These structural differences may be a result of a specific articulation of modes of production which has capitalism as the dominant mode of production. This method of proceeding encounters the difficulties of situating 'internal' and 'external' factors in a coherent theoretical framework. An alternative to this approach is to treat the structures of dependency not as the result of a specific articulation of modes of production but as a mode of production in itself, *sui generis*.

This last approach has the advantage that the different laws of motion of the dependent economy are to be expected. It has the great drawback, however, of being very unspecific as to the precise nature of this new mode of production. It is all very well to give it a label, but how does it work? Until someone comes up with a convincing model of the operation of such a mode of production, we must conclude 'not proven'.

A central difficulty with the attempt to describe dependency as a mode of production is that, apparently, as a mode of production it cannot exist in pure form, in isolation from other modes of production, since it depends on the existence of advanced capitalism for its continued operation.

An additional caution is that just as it has been necessary to differentiate between the kind of dependency that might exist between metropolitan nations, and the kind of dependency that exists in the Third World, so also one might hesitate to use the same term to describe, say, Brazil and Bolivia. Of course, there may be several dependent modes of production in the periphery, and this cannot be ruled out *a priori*; nevertheless it would seem more prudent to reserve judgement.

Must we then return to the notion of dependency as a social formation defined by the complex articulation, both internal and external, of several modes of production? It seems that we must. But it should be pointed out that it is neither the *complexity* of the articulation, nor the *multiplicity* of the modes of production being articulated, that results in continued backwardness; but rather the specific manner in which this articulation is achieved. The particular articulations characteristic of dependent societies are not foreordained. They are the result of an historical process of imperialist domination. The result is that the different modes of production are articulated in such a way as either to discourage growth, or to transfer the benefits of growth abroad. Industry is owned by foreigners who remit potentially investible surplus; domestic entrepreneurs are disinclined to invest and prefer to spend money on luxury consumption, etc. This is the old catalogue of the vices of underdevelopment. These are the well-known 'obstacles' to development which have provided the bulk of the literature on development before the dependency paradigm became popular. What then has been added?

One approach to this question has been to emphasise the role played by merchant capital in underdeveloped countries. Kay, Rey and Amin have all argued that the expanding world capitalist economy first articulated with the peripheral economies by creating a class of merchant capitalists (Kay, 1975; Amin, 1976; Rey, 1976). This class ensured the transfer of the commodities of the Third World to the developed capitalist countries at a rate of exchange favourable to the latter, but did not itself engage in, or organise, the production process itself. Production was carried on by pre-capitalist methods (unless a foreign corporation began production in an enclave). The consolidation of merchant capital, and the dominance of this class, proved to be an obstacle to the emergence of a real industrial bourgeoisie which would reorganise production along capitalist lines.

For some theorists, such as Rey, this ossification of underdevelopment under the aegis of merchant capital is but a way-station on the route to modern capitalism. The differences occur in the early stages, particularly in the alleged need of the colonial power to break the resistance of the pre-capitalist modes of production by violence. Because of the differences in the starting point, and because capitalism was introduced from the outside the transition will have distinct characteristics. But it will still be a transition to the same end-state, modern capitalism.

A different position has been to emphasise the way in which the dependent economy was disarticulated by the impact of imperialism, and then its various parts reintegrated with the metropolitan economy. This is most obvious in the case of mineral-exporting enclave economies, but it could be argued that the proposition is generally true for all underdeveloped countries. However, before accepting such a proposition, a typology of forms of disarticulation/ reintegration would have to be developed.

Whatever version of dependency analysis we accept, it remains true that the dependency paradigm alerts us to the fact that much-needed reforms are impossible without a restructuring of the mode of articulation of the economy with the world economy. Most dependency theorists argue that this restructuring will be opposed by the ruling class in the dependent country and by imperialism, and that this resistance will only be overcome by a revolution. The dependency paradigm argues that the only realistic alternatives are revolution or continued dependency.

Perhaps there seems to be a disproportion between the energy expended in the debate and the results achieved; a lot of heat and very little light. We sympathise with O'Brien when he says,

> Dependency is undoubtedly here to stay. The basic point it makes – that the interplay between the internal Latin American structures and international structures is the critical starting point for an understanding of the process of development in Latin America – is of vital importance. But was it really necessary to write so many millions of words to establish just this perspective? (O'Brien, 1975, p. 25)

Our answer is yes, unfortunately it was necessary. The transition from one paradigm to another demands a tremendous effort of conversion. In the social sciences, themselves an arena for contending ideologies, where the simple statement of the 'obvious' becomes a direct challenge to the ideological legitimation of imperialist domination, this is even more the case.

6

Social Structure

The term 'class' is a hotly contested one in contemporary social thought. There are many definitions, and much disagreement even among Marxists as to the meaning of the term. There will be no attempt at theoretical rigour in this book, nor will there be an attempt to discuss the various theories which have been put forward. Instead we will limit ourselves to a few cursory remarks.

In the first place, class is a relationship between two sets of people. It is a way of behaving which characterises social aggregates. As such it is embodied in institutions and is formed historically. What distinguishes class from other forms of social aggregation are its structural underpinnings. The basis of class relations are the relations between men in the productive process. The social relations of production, which divide men into direct producers and those who appropriate the fruits of their labour, are the starting point for a definition of class. The ways in which men respond to this structured manner of producing material goods constitute class relations.

Clearly, the way the production relations are seen by those involved in them, and the kinds of institutions and social practices which grow up around them, contain within them an inherently large range of variability. Thus the same class situation (that is, the 'objective' relations of production) can give rise to quite distinct forms of class practice and class consciousness. Classes *are* these forms of historically constituted social practice and shared feelings and perceptions. One is not more 'subjective' or 'objective' than the other. Class, class action and class consciousness are simply different facets of a single, if complex, social relationship.

There is, however, a dualism between class situation and class, so that it is not possible mechanically to read off class behaviour or class consciousness (what we are here calling 'class') from the distribution of work roles and property relations. The same distribution of work roles and property relations could give rise to significantly different class structures because classes are formed historically in a continual process of conflict and accommodation.

However, to say that there is a range of possible variation, is not to say by any means that the relationship is either arbitrary or unknowable. Quite to the contrary, many significant statements can be made about the relationships between the organisation of economic activity and the process of class formation. The point is simply that there is not a simple, one-way, 100 per cent determination of one by the other. The process of class formation occurs in a complex way, so that class, race, religion, politics, all are inextricably interwoven in the structure of any given class society.

The perceptions men have of themselves in class societies are determined in large part by their experience of conflict with other classes. This being the case, if we can specify conflicts which are structurally located in a given type of society, we can go some way to predicting the ways in which classes will form and the kinds of action that they will undertake to pursue. For some classes in some societies we can meaningfully talk of a 'class project'; that is, an historically grounded vision of itself, its place in society, and a vision of a future society, together with a more or less defined programme of action to implement this change. In this sense, to the degree that a class possesses this vision, this class project, it can be considered to be an historical actor. This is, of course, a matter of degree; no class is ever entirely lacking in consciousness of its position in society, though the nature of this consciousness may vary greatly.

A distinction ought to be made between historical classes which have potentially hegemonic class projects and classes which cannot conceive of another form of society, and must therefore always play a secondary role in any class struggle. (Secondary in the sense that they have no project of their own; they either follow some other class's project or implement that project, on behalf of that class.) In Marxist analysis, both the urban petty bourgeoisie and the peasantry are classes which cannot realistically reorganise society on their own terms. Their world views must always contain utopian elements. (This distinction between historic classes and non-historic classes is not the same as the distinction between hegemonic and subordinate, or between dominant and dominated classes.)

One difficulty which follows from the use of the notion of class discussed above is that much of the data which is available has been organised and collected for other concepts. Although data on income distribution, occupational structure, property relations, etc., have some bearing on the analysis of social class, they provide at best a series of approximations which illustrate only partial aspects of social class. Such bodies of data must therefore be treated with due caution, and it would be unwise to draw inferences as to political behaviour directly from them.

The class structures of the Third World differ from those of the advanced nations in two principal ways: they are more complex, and the classes themselves are usually much weaker. In the first place, the rural sector is of immense importance in the Third World.

Modern social theory has been almost exclusively concerned with urban social classes and, with the dwindling of the size of the rural population in the developed countries, sociological interest has also declined, except in so far as rural folk provide the material for studies of peripheral and marginal aspects of social processes. In the Third World, however, rural class structures vary greatly from one country or region to another, and some rural class structures are quite complex in themselves. I will discuss some of the complexities in the following chapter. In addition, it is often in the rural arena that some of the most profound changes are taking place. As a result, the rural class structure is often a composite of two or more class structures, corresponding to different 'moments' of social change.

But if the rural class structure is often highly fluid and in the process of change, the urban class structure is frequently of recent formation. Urban classes are recently formed and in the process of continuous and rapid change. The urban working class, for example, has in many countries recently come from the countryside and has not yet formed itself as an exclusively urban class. Many recently-arrived workers still maintain close links with their rural place of origin.

Sociologists have been greatly impressed with the fact of rural origins of the new urban lower classes, and some have used this as a major explanatory device, arguing that the urban lower classes are really 'peasants in the city' (Mangin, 1970). We will return to this point shortly in the section where we discuss the urban lower classes in more detail.

Not only are the class structures of the underdeveloped nations complex and weak, they are frequently 'incomplete' in the sense that the dominant class, or one fraction of the dominant class, is absent. This is the case where the dominant class or fraction thereof is foreign, and does not directly form part of the legitimate structures of the nation-state. For example, the bourgeoisie of the United States, or some part of it, such as a multinational corporation, might confront working classes in several countries in terms of an immediate and direct class struggle, yet not be directly represented in any of those countries. This kind of class struggle, which transcends the boundaries of nation-states, is perhaps a good argument for not focusing on the nation-state as a unit of analysis, and talking instead, as writers like Samir Amin do, of a single world class structure. Nevertheless, it seems preferable to argue that whilst certain dominant classes may compose themselves historically at a global level, this is not true of any other class. All other classes are formed at a local, or most usually, national level. (Since the state tends to be the arena in which classes are organised politically, it is not at all surprising that classes should be formed at the national level.)

Lastly, common to all class structures is the fact that non-property based structures of conflict such as race, religion and language, interact with cleavages derived from the economic sphere to prevent a simple crystallisation of class conflict along property lines. While this is true of all countries, the development of capitalism in the West has had (with the possible exception of the United States) an homogenising effect, so that such non-economic cleavages have become increasingly less important. In the countries of the Third World, these 'secondary' lines of conflict are, however, often very important.

When all these contradictions are present in the colonial or neo-colonial situation, it is quite legitimate to ask, what is the 'principal contradiction'? Is it the conflict between the nation and the foreign oppressor, or is it the internal conflict between social classes? Of course, the anti-imperialist conflict can be, and ought to be, analysed in terms of class alliances, and it is of considerable importance to find out exactly which class leads the struggle, and what kind of settlement will be effected after independence. Nevertheless, the conflict between the nation and the external oppressor is still a real conflict which is not reducible to a form of class struggle in every instance. Since nation-states form the basis for political organisation, conflict among states has a reality, a level of effectivity, of its own, and there is a very real sense in which any state represents the people, even if its notion of what constitutes 'the national interest' is one which is structured by an immediate class interest.

The complexity of the class structure means that a greater variety of forms of class alliance is possible. For example, if we take a simple four-class model with an urban upper class (bourgeoisie) and lower class (proletariat), and a rural upper class (landed oligarchy) and lower class (peasantry), we can see that, at least in formal terms, the lines of the class conflict can be drawn in a number of ways. For example, the two lower classes could form a worker–peasant alliance and struggle against a reactionary alliance of the bourgeoisie and landed oligarchy. Or, in the Communist Party's version of the 'progressive national bourgeoisie', that class may join together with both the peasantry and the proletariat against the reactionary landed oligarchy. Alternatively, the urban bourgeoisie may join forces with the proletariat to defend their sectoral interests as industrial producers *vis-à-vis* agriculture, demanding, for example, lower prices for foodstuffs and higher prices for manufactured goods. In this sectoral conflict the urban classes may be opposed to an alliance of peasants and landowners, or the landed oligarchy may be able to avoid direct conflict with the urban sector by passing the cost of the new arrangement directly on to the peasantry.

Which form of conflict actually occurs in any given historical situation cannot be decided in the abstract; it will depend on a variety of factors, both structural and conjunctural.

Naturally, this four-class model is an extremely simplified version of what might happen. A more refined analysis would distinguish between fractions of the bourgeoisie, would incorporate the middle classes and petty bourgeoisie, and would make distinctions within the lower class between the labour aristocracy and the lumpenproletariat. In the rural sector, the various types of peasantry would be distinguished. These distinctions are neither arbitrary nor universal; it is a question of which classes do actually exist in any specific country. Moreover, the way in which these various classes find expression politically would have to be considered at length.

Nevertheless, despite the apparent complexity which has just been introduced into the analysis, certain kinds of generalisations can be made. Barrington Moore, for example, has argued that in the transition to the modern world, which of three possible paths (democracy, revolution from above, or revolution from below) is taken by an underdeveloped society depends in large part on the response of the landed upper class to the commercialisation of agriculture. This enables him to provide a structural analysis of how the differing forms of class conflict have predictable political consequences. There are certain problems with Moore's analysis. One, which has been mentioned in Chapter 2, is that the analysis is only applicable to large societies undergoing a process of more or less endogenous change. A second problem concerns the nature of the key variable, the response of the landed upper class to the commercialisation of agriculture. It is a highly subjective notion, and is itself largely unexplained in structural terms. (Other similar instances occur in his treatment of the relationship between the landlord and the peasantry, and this will be mentioned in the following chapter.)

In addition to making generalisations about the probable consequences of particular forms of class alliance and class conflict, it is also possible to investigate the conditions which will tend to produce certain kinds of class conflict. For example, in the case of Latin America, it might be suggested, following Frank, that whenever the ties between the centre and the periphery are loosened, and the conditions for industrial development appear, it is likely that the domestic bourgeoisie will form a progressive alliance with the working class against the landed oligarchy. In other words, the behaviour of the world economy at a given point will create the conditions in certain kinds of underdeveloped societies which will predispose the bourgeoisie to form certain kinds of class alliance. Whether or not this actually happens will depend on a number of other factors, many of which will be conjunctural or even accidental.

Having said this, it is then possible to examine the probable political consequences of this class alliance. In the context of ISI, such a class alliance would probably, with a new and weak working class, produce a variety of populism, with the working class making certain concrete gains in terms of improved real wages and strengthened trade union organisations, but nevertheless being clearly a subordinate partner in the class alliance, and having its political organisations structured by the state so as to prevent the development of autonomous working-class organisation. This seems to have been the case in Brazil in the 1930s, and although similar phenomena appear to have occurred in both Argentina and Chile at the same time, the prior organisation and development of the working class, as a class, precluded populist forms of ideological mobilisation, even though in the case of Argentina the independence of the working class as a social force was concealed by the populist elements of Peronist organisation and ideology – concealed even from many members of the working class themselves (Little, 1975).

An assumption underlying the previous discussion of classes and class alliances – and which also underlies a great deal of theorising, such as Barrington Moore's – is that the landed oligarchy and the industrial bourgeoisie constitute two distinct social classes. This is also the case with much Marxist theorising, which asserts that the landed oligarchy are the representatives of feudalism in the countryside, whereas the industrial bourgeoisie is formed as a result of capitalist relations of production in the cities. This clear distinction between the two upper classes may indeed correspond to historical reality, but this needs to be demonstrated empirically.

For at least some countries, available evidence casts doubt on the assertion that there are two distinct upper classes. In both Brazil and Chile for example, research has suggested that the family groups of industrialists and agriculturalists overlap considerably so that members of the same family have interests both in industry and in agriculture. Indeed, this may also be true of individuals. The overlapping of economic interests among kinship groups does suggest that it may be more appropriate in such cases to refer to a single class which is sufficiently homogenous to prevent the identification of separate and distinct fractions (Zeitlin et al., 1974; Dean, 1969). In such a case, political representation may be exceedingly complex (Zeitlin et al., 1976). In the Chilean case, for example, it was frequently asserted that the National Party represented the interests of an agrarian oligarchy whereas the Christian Democratic Party represented the interests of the industrial bourgeoisie. The conflict between the National Party and the Christian Democratic Party over the agrarian reform of the 1960s (which involved the expropriation of many of the great estates of the

Central Valley) was interpreted as a direct expression of class conflict. Similarly, the conflicts over the prices of agricultural and industrial goods which have characterised Chilean politics since the 1930s were also seen as expressions of an obvious class conflict. However, this line of analysis, appealing though it is, does not square with the evidence produced by Maurice Zeitlin about the unitary nature of the Chilean upper class. If Zeitlin's evidence is accepted, then these explanations which link political representation directly to class interest must be discarded in favour of a more complex approach. This alternative approach would see the competition between the two parties as representing two alternative visions of bourgeois development open to the Chilean upper class. It would suggest that the Chilean upper class was faced with some kind of choice about the nature of its development programme and that the competition between the two parties reflected this. In the Chilean case political fractions would not, therefore, directly correspond to economic fractions.

The conclusion to be drawn is not that in every underdeveloped country there will always be a unitary upper class. In many countries the upper class may well be split into two or more fractions or distinct classes. But whether this is so must always be problematic, and the relationship between economic interest and political representation must also be taken as problematic. There may be a direct correspondence, or there may not.

If there are difficulties with the analysis of the upper classes, then the middle classes present an even greater problem. The conceptual and theoretical confusions surrounding analyses of the upper classes are minor compared to those surrounding the analysis of their less well-off emulators.

In some analyses, the term 'middle class' simply displaces the notion of bourgeoisie, and the middle classes are seen as rivals and opponents of the 'elites' or oligarchies. As such, the middle classes become a surrogate in orthodox sociological analysis for the Communist Party concept of a progressive national bourgeoisie. The history of the underdeveloped countries is seen as the history of the rise of the middle classes. They either, in the recently colonised countries, displace the colonial elites, or in the countries such as Latin America which have been formally independent for some time, they displace the old agrarian elites.

They thus become the bearers of progress and democracy. This process started in Latin America, according to one proponent of this thesis, J. J. Johnson, during the phase of ISI in the 1930s (Johnson, 1958). This may not occur by way of a direct replacement of one class by another. The middle classes, because of their weak internal organisation as a class, may not assume power directly. Instead, the army may act as a surrogate for the middle classes, ousting the old elites for them and ruling on their behalf (Nún, 1967; Huntington, 1968).

One central problem with this analysis is the failure to distinguish between the bourgeoisie as such and the middle classes. This is closely tied up with the vagueness with which the concept is defined. Johnson acknowledges this, and claims that the vagueness of the concept simply reflects the reality. He says:

> the terms 'middle sectors', 'middle groups', 'middle segments', 'middle components', 'middle elements', used interchangeably, were settled upon to convey the idea of 'middleness' without paralelling any fixed criteria of 'middleness' employed in areas outside Latin America. (Johnson, 1958, p. ix)

> Clearly, the middle sectors are anything but a compact social layer. They do not fulfill the central condition of a class: their members have no common background of experience. (Johnson, 1958, p. 3)

We really need to ask whether the middle class is one class or several. There are at least four fractions or classes which could be labelled 'middle class'. There are the lower ranks of the bourgeoisie which should really be considered as belonging to the bourgeoisie. There is an urban professional class which can reasonably be called 'middle class'. There is an indistinct class which forms around political roles and managerial positions in the nationalised industries. This one might call the state petty bourgeoisie, or even the state bourgeoisie. Finally, there is a class of street traders and small entrepreneurs, shopkeepers, artisans, etc., who own small amounts of capital but work it mainly on their own or with the labour of their families. This group can reasonably be called petty bourgeoisie, and should generally be distinguished from the small bourgeoisie. (White-collar workers we treat as part of the working class.)

Generally speaking, these four classes will form themselves into distinct classes and will exist in most social formations in the Third World. Their relative size will vary, of course, from one country to another. They will frequently be found in political alliance with one another, and many of their political responses will be sufficiently similar to justify treating them as an undifferentiated bloc. However, one should never lose sight of the great degree of heterogeneity which actually exists.

Whether one or more of these disparate elements which are lumped together under the common label of middle class is in some sense progressive, needs to be discussed. The appeal of such an analysis is, of course, great. It resonates well the distortions of Weber's analysis of the Protestant ethic, in which a search is made for some modern and ascetic group which will strive hard to accumulate and develop a work ethic, and the middle classes with their 'modern' consumption patterns seem to be the bearers of 'modern values' *par excellence*. And the notion that the middle classes are the bearers of progress provides a useful ideological counterweight to the traditional Marxist assumption that they would be ground out of existence between the millstones of the bourgeoisie and the proletariat.

Unfortunately for these theories, the evidence that the middle classes are progressive in an historical sense is ambiguous. In the early phases of development, they may indeed put forward progressive demands, but once a threat of socialism appears from their left, from an independently organised and autonomous working class, then they close ranks with the bourgeoisie behind a principled defence of capital.

In Latin America, for example, in the period of ISI in the 1930s, the middle-class parties were generally to the left of centre, only to turn in the 1950s and 1960s to the defence of the institutional order against threats of revolution from below. In Chile the radicalism of the middle classes was sustained up until the 1970s by the Radical and Christian Democratic parties, though with the installation of the Marxist, Allende, in the presidency, they rapidly became the social forces which undermined and finally brought down the regime. Similarly, in Brazil, despite their support for the industrialising policies of Vargas in the 1930s, the middle classes vociferously demanded the ouster of Goulart in 1964 as he tried to implement a policy of structural reforms couched in the rhetoric of populism. And in Cuba, the middle classes were so closely identified with the goals of the revolution during the early stages of Fidel Castro's rule that many observers saw the increasing distance between Castro and the middle class as a 'betrayal' of what had been essentially a middle-class revolution. The same might be said of the Bolivian revolution of 1952.

Thus, although in many countries of the Third World the petty bourgeoisie and the middle classes appear early on the political stage as the leaders of movements for independence and economic development, the course of events sooner or later brings them into conflict with their previous allies and they turn increasingly to the repressive powers of the state to bolster their position. In time, this process may entail the transformation of the middle classes into a new bourgeoisie, possibly a state bourgeoisie. I leave this issue until the final chapter.

Moving further down the social scale we come to the urban working class. In most underdeveloped countries, the wage-earning proletariat of the cities is small compared to other social classes, particularly when compared to the peasantry. It is also often of recent formation. The working class is also sharply divided in terms of the kind of establishments in which they work. Three different kinds of workplace may be distinguished. Up to 50 per cent or more of the workforce is employed by small establishments of less than ten workers. At the other end of the scale some big multinational or state enterprises employ thousands of workers in modern industrial settings. The third type of employment situation for industrial workers is in the mineral-extracting enclaves, if they exist. These may well be situated hundreds of miles from the major urban centres.

The working class is, of course, also stratified according to skill levels and educational attainments. Given the high levels of unemployment, these factors often work together to produce a dual labour market in which the mass of unskilled workers compete for casual and badly-paid labour, while a smaller group of relatively skilled workers have stable jobs in the modern and large enterprises with relatively high wages and usually are well organised into unions. While this group enjoys a relatively secure bargaining position within the labour market, the vast mass of the workers are faced with weak bargaining positions and the threat of unemployment. This is aggravated by the rapid urbanisation of the major cities of the Third World. One expression of this massive drift to the cities is the proliferation of the so-called tertiary sector. This tertiary sector includes all forms of urban services, from professionals like lawyers and doctors to street vendors and office workers. Many of the people who fall into this catch-all category are paid very little and their productivity is extremely low. Their contribution to the growth of the economy is minimal, and they are often in some form or other of disguised unemployment. (Or they may work as servants of the upper income strata, providing luxury services at cheap rates.) And the number of directly unemployed is often very high. As we noted in Chapter 3, this high level of unemployment and disguised unemployment is in part a consequence of the capital-intensive technology which is favoured by the multinational corporations.

This hiatus in the workforce has led some analysts to describe the better-off section of the urban proletariat as a 'labour aristocracy'. The implication is that the economically privileged position of this group sets it apart from the rest of the class and produces a politically conservative defence of its privileged position. There is a certain amount of confusion behind the term 'labour aristocracy'. It may refer to a stratum of workers who earn high incomes *per se*. Secondly, it could be used to refer to a stratum of workers whose incomes are high with respect to the rest of the lower classes or the rest of the urban working class. The third sense in which the term might be employed, and the one which is closest to Lenin's original meaning, is to refer to a stratum of workers who earn high incomes because they are receiving colonial tribute in one form or another.

However the term is used, the evidence to support the conclusion that there existed a labour aristocracy with conservative political views is not strong even in the history of the countries of Western Europe which provide the basis for the theory in the first place. The link between income and politics is too direct for us not to be suspicious of it. In the first place, one must ask whether these workers in highly paid and well organised jobs actually constitute a separate class or fraction of a class. For the working class as a whole, we need to look at things such as the recency of rural–urban migration, the stability of employment, the nature of unemployment, the types of occupational mobility structures which are operative in any given society (Balán, 1973; Dore, 1973).

We need to look at residential and associational patterns, and occupational mobility within the working class. Above all, we need to analyse the life histories of members of the workforce to see to what extent they move from one kind of employment to another, and to what extent occupational life-chances are shared by members of the same family or community.

The historical evidence does not immediately support the proposition that there exists an easily identifiable labour aristocracy. In Chile, for example, the nitrate and copper miners of the northern deserts – the obvious candidates for a labour aristocracy – were always industrially militant and were early supporters of the left-wing parties. In Brazil and Argentina the historical record suggests that the working class as a whole supported the populist leadership of Peron and Vargas (and later Goulart), at least, when those leaders were fulfilling their share of the bargain and delivering the goods in the form of higher wages.

But if it would be erroneous to describe the working class, or any section of it, as politically conservative, equal caution should be taken with attempts to describe it as always progressive or revolutionary. The political stance adopted by a class at any given time will be in part a function of the structure of the political system as a whole and the concrete possibilities which exist in a specific situation for the application of various kinds of class alliances. This will depend in part on the historical development of the forms of political parties (and in more general terms, the relationship between narrowly economic and broadly political struggles), the nature of the political tradition of the working class, whether it has a reformist or populist heritage, and the kind of class alliance which is entered into.

Very few useful statements can be made about the political orientations of any social class or aggregate in a vacuum: only by situating the analysis in a specific historical context can we begin to make reasonable statements about likely political behaviour (Mouzelis, 1978).

At the other end of the scale from the labour aristocracy is the lumpenproletariat, the shanty-town dwellers, the 'marginalised' elements who live in the *favelas* and *bidonvilles*. More so than the labour aristocracy, these people have been the focus of a great deal of research. Some analysts have seen these people as a lumpen-proletariat, vicious, idle and reactionary. Fresh from the countryside, these immigrants to the big cities form a disorganised and poverty-stricken mass, given to crime and all forms of deviance. Variously labelled as 'anomic', 'alienated' or 'marginal', they are seen as a disposable mass, available for political mobilisation by charismatic leaders.

This kind of mass theory of politics, which finds its clearest expression in Kornhauser's book, *The Politics of Mass Society*, argues that when the intermediate level of social structures are broken down or eroded by rapid social change, then there is nothing between the individual and the play of social forces (Kornhauser, 1959). Consequently, in a direct development of the Durkheimian tradition, the individual is seen as anomic, cut off from the guiding institutions of the church, family and rural community which had acted as buffers between him and the wider society and had given him a sense of his place in the world. Once this 'massification' has set in, it is but a short step to bring in the Weberian notion of a charismatic leader who will be able to mobilise these available masses. This theoretical framework has been used to attempt to explain the rise of Nazism and Communism, and variations on the theme are used to explain populism in underdeveloped countries and the politics of the 'marginal mass'.

These marginals were seen, then, by the defenders of the established order as a potential threat, a potential revolutionary force. This analysis had its leftist equivalent in the Jacobinism of Franz Fanon, who believed that the 'wretched of the earth' would prove to be the motor force behind decolonisation and the construction of socialism in the countries of the Third World (Fanon, 1967).

However, the years passed and the wretched of the earth neglected to take up the banner of human emancipation. A re-examination of these theories (theories which had come from the centre of sociological theorising about underdevelopment) was due. Initially, the re-thinking led to two distinct reactions. On the one hand, some theorists were loath to abandon such a promising theory, and modified it with the 'second generation hypothesis'. If the first generation of rural migrants had failed to display the signs of radicalism, this was because they still carried with them the old rural values of deference and passivity. Their children, however, the second generation of shanty-town dwellers, would have new reference groups and would be socialised into new sets of values and expectations. They would experience immense frustration and this would be translated into aggression which could be directed against the prevailing political order.

The second reaction was to deny that the migrants would ever be politically radical. On the basis of some anthropological studies of shanty-towns, which stressed the degree to which their inhabitants created social bonds, it was argued that they would be politically passive. This version accepted the basic theoretical framework, but argued that the move to the big city did not automatically entail the destruction of community ties. Rather, the migrants re-created new versions of their previous rural community networks once they arrived in the city. The occupations of land on which shanty-towns would be built, it was noted, were highly organised, the inhabitants displayed high solidarity with each other, and were all interested in various kinds of self-improvement, of which the gradual construction of a decent house was the most visible sign. When questioned, they proved not to be disaffected marginals, but instead accepted the dominant values of the society. Home ownership and democracy, the magic couple of conservative social thought, seemed to be working its miracle just as it had in the West (Perlman, 1976).

These reworkings of the theory certainly represented an advance on the unsophisticated and apocalyptic vision of an imminent ava-lanche of radical mobs, but were still predicated on some seriously erroneous assumptions. All these versions presented an implicit picture of an harmonious village community which was almost certainly seriously exaggerated. Peasant life, as we shall see in the next chapter, was not all bread and roses.

Moreover, the peasants-in-the-city version tended, in an under-standable reaction against the previous theory, to exaggerate the degree of solidarity and community which actually existed in many shanty-towns; the available evidence was by no means unequivoc-able on this point.

Clearly the matter was (and is) more complex. At least three elements in the analysis which had been treated in a relatively unproblematic fashion needed to be examined more closely. The nature of the migration process from countryside to city, and the relevance of this for political socialisation had to be examined in more detail. The variations in the types of urban settlement to which the migrants moved had to be clearly recognised. And the way in which the 'marginals' were articulated with the political and economic systems had to be spelt out in more detail. It simply was not the case that they were excluded from the wider society. On the contrary, they were integrated in to the larger social structure in a variety of ways, but on disadvantageous terms. We will now examine these three issues in more detail.

If we look at the question of rural–urban migration, we see that, in the first place, many of the so-called marginals were born in big cities. As time goes on, this will of course become a more important phenomenon, but it has rarely been negligible. Secondly, it is not always the case that migrants come directly from the rural environment to the capital city. They may come via a succession of steps, from countryside to the village, and then on to the town, the city and finally the metropolis. This kind of stepwise migration (which may undergo several permutations) might allow for a gradual introduction of the migrant into urban ways of life. Whether direct or stepwise migration occurs depends on a variety of factors, but the evidence from Mexico, for example, suggests that in the early phases of urbanisation, stepwise migration is important, whereas in the later phases, migration directly from the countryside to the capital city is likely to be predominant. This historical switch means that the transition is eased for the early waves of migrants, and they have the possibility of making a gradual adjustment to city ways, whereas the later waves, who do not have the chance of a gradual adjustment, come to urban settlements which are already established and are able to fit into an already-formed social category.

In some parts of the world, besides the kind of permanent migration discussed above, there are various forms of temporary migration. This may be seasonal, or a stage in a life-cycle. These returning migrants may be less affected by urban values, but to the extent that they are, they act as socialising agents in their home communities. Then too, migration is often selective, in the sense that the cream of the rural population tend to migrate; particularly young and educated men. While this tends to increase the skill levels in the community to which the migrants go, it tends to have detrimental effects in their place of origin. In considering the kind of migrant that arrives in the big city, differences in the communities of origin need to be taken into consideration. As we shall see in the following chapter, rural social structures exhibit a high degree of variability.

A final consideration in discussing rural–urban migration is to distinguish the type of community to which the migrant goes. This leads us directly to the next issue; that of the need to develop a typology of urban settlements.

There is a striking difference between the inner-city slums and the shanty-towns on the outskirts of the city. The slums may indeed be centres of misery and poverty, disorganised and anomic. But they represent only a small part of the picture. By contrast with the inner-city slums, the shanty-towns tend to be more stable and socially integrated communities. Alejandro Portes has suggested a typology of urban settlements which distinguishes between temporary and permanent housing, and whether the intiative for the settlement was popular or government-originated. By crossing these two variables, he generates a fourfold typology (Portes, 1971) – see Table 2. Only the slum fits the marginality stereotype.

TABLE 2   *Types of low-income settlement*

	Popular initiative	*Government*	.
Temporary	Slum	Decaying housing project	
Permanent	Squatter settlement	New resettlement area	

SOURCE   Portes (1971).

The question is, of course, who lives in these settlements? To treat a category of people as a social class simply and exclusively on the basis of their residential location – as has been done by nearly all writers who theorise about the politics of the shanty-town dwellers – is quite inadequate. It is often assumed that the inhabitants of these shanty-towns are either unemployed or engaged in various forms of low-paid tertiary employment. Whether they are described as a lumpenproletariat, as marginals, as a sub-proletariat or whatever, it is assumed that these people constitute a separate social class in some easily identifiable sense.

This is questionable. It is true, of course, that unemployment is high. But data from Chile indicate that very high proportions of the populations of these shanty-towns are, in fact, industrial workers. The shanty-towns are, in fact, the places where the working class lives. Of course, not everyone in the shanty-town is an industrial worker; but nor are they all 'lumpen'. Quite what the occupational composition is, and what the occupational life-histories of the inhabitants are, and how the various occupational groups interact in the context of the shanty-town to form a social class, are all important questions on which very little empirical social research has been done. But what is clear is that some settlements are really working-class neighbourhoods. Castells has suggested that if settlements are differentiated according to income and occupation then four distinct social compositions may be discerned (Castells, 1971) – see Table 3.

TABLE 3 *Class composition of shanty-towns*

	Lumpen	Proletariat in crisis I	Proletariat in crisis II	White collar and petty bourgeois
Income	Low	Low	Relatively high	Relatively high
Occupation	Self-employed	Manual	Manual	Self-employed or white collar

SOURCE Castells (1971).

The point is that it is not possible to take a residential category and treat this as though one were dealing with an homogenous and undifferentiated social class. Residential location and class membership do not always overlap completely, even in situations in which we are dealing with stable and coherent social classes. In the Third World, where social classes are often still in the process of formation, to treat residential categories as a surrogate for social classes is even more misleading.

The third issue follows from this consideration. The articulation of the shanty-town dwellers with the larger political and economic systems is problematic for two principal reasons. In the first place, the political behaviour of any class, group or category is not an inherent function of the class itself, but rather a result of its interaction with other classes in the context of the overall political system. Therefore, one cannot say 'the military will be radical', or 'the peasants will be conservative' or 'the marginals will be a source of revolutionary support' in general terms. One can only say, 'in such-and-such a political system with such-and-such characteristics, then an historically defined social class with such-and-such characteristics may be expected to behave in this or that manner'. All sociological propositions must be of this conditional form. In the second place, we are dealing with a heterogeneous social force; hence, it will inevitably display inconsistent behaviour.

In terms of the way in which the 'marginal' population are articulated with the economy, there are broadly speaking three positions which have been advanced. The first position holds that the marginals are the working class together with the reserve army of labour. In this version, there is no basic difference between the Third World and the already industrialised countries in this respect. It is argued that the service or 'informal' sector provides cheap inputs into the modern sector and is therefore to be considered simply as part of the capitalist division of labour.

The second line of reasoning argues that the unemployment in the Third World is far greater than Marx had in mind when he talked about the reserve army of labour. The reserve army of labour served the function, in Marx's analysis, of keeping wages down to an historically given subsistence level. It could be argued, the proponents of this view assert, that unemployment in the Third World could be substantially reduced without raising wages above the subsistence minimum. In this sense, the high levels of unemployment in the Third World are dysfunctional even in terms of the operation of a capitalist economy and these theorists have therefore argued that the marginals are to be regarded as an historically new category (Nún, 1969). Against this it has been suggested that Marx's analysis was not carried out in functional terms, but in terms of contradiction, and that the criterion of the 'functional' level of unemployment implicitly employed in these discussions is methodologically quite illegitimate.

This third position appears superficially to be similar to the second, but in methodological terms it is quite distinct and does not lay itself open to these charges of functionalism. The third position, exemplified by Quijano, argues that the marginals are participants in a different mode of production, a non-capitalist mode of production, which is described variously as a petty-commodity mode of production or, in different terms, as the 'informal sector'. It is argued that this petty-commodity mode of production is articulated with the dominant capitalist mode of production in such a way as to facilitate the expanded reproduction of the capitalist mode of production (Quijano, 1974).

What the politics of the 'underclass' might be – if indeed it
is a new social class – remain to be specified. Dale Johnson has
argued that the oligarchies, middle strata and the working class
rest upon the internally colonised and the underclasses:

> Structurally all these classes rest upon ... the colonised and
> those who escape the colonial situation to become part of an
> underclass of unemployed or casually employed laborers crowded
> into squalid urban slums. (Johnson, 1973, p. 30)

Is this just a figure of speech, or is the implication that this
structural differentiation entails political conflict between the underclasses and what, for want of a better neologism, we might call
the 'overclasses'? According to Dale Johnson, one of the characteristics of the underclasses is that they are in some sense marginal.

> Marginal underclasses are those populations which have not
> been integrated, or have been integrated under highly disadvanta-
> geous conditions into the institutions of society, but are not
> located in what will be termed 'regionally based internal colonies'
> or of allegedly inferior or cultural origins. Categorised by the
> character of participation in the economy, these include the
> hard-core unemployed, those employed in low-wage sectors and
> ... those whose skills are superfluous to a technologically geared
> society. (Johnson, 1972, p. 276)

The suggestion seems to be that the working class, for example,
since it is not part of the marginal underclasses, is *not* integrated
into the institutions of society under highly disadvantageous conditions. It is presumably integrated into society under advantageous
conditions. One would expect this sort of conservative analysis
to resonate well in the works of the ideological guardians of the
status quo. That a self-professed revolutionary holds such views calls
for some explanation.

The justification for treating this heterogeneous mass of unemployed, partly-employed and poor people as a special category
resides in the different mechanisms used to keep wages low. In
the classical capitalism described by Marx, the function of keeping
wages low was performed by the reserve army of labour. For

this purpose, the absolute size of the reserve army need not be very large. All the evidence suggests that unemployment and under-employment in Third World countries is above this level. Moreover, only a small percentage of the unemployed or partially employed ever join the ranks of the industrial proletariat. Because the social formations of the Third World are distinct, we cannot treat these categories of people simply as a reserve army of labour. This does not mean that they are necessarily dysfunctional for the oper-ation of the economic system. They perform essential roles in the system and in this sense are not marginal at all.

It could, perhaps, be argued that these underclasses are marginal in the sense that they do not participate in the system (Gonzalez-Casanova, 1970, p. 71). To be more precise, they do not benefit from the fruits of progress. The marginal are the poor, the illiterate, etc. The concept becomes entirely descriptive; the marginal are the poor.

This, however, is not what the term 'underclass' is meant to convey: it is meant to suggest a link between structural location and political potential. Not the proletariat, but the marginal masses are the force for social change in the Third World. This is scarcely a new notion. What is important about it is that it follows directly from the way in which Frank and his co-workers use the concept of class.

Unlike the Marxist view of class, the Frankian view of class conceptualises not merely exploiting classes and exploited classes, but also classes which are at one and the same time both exploiting and exploited. In Frank's framework, every class between the pea-sant at the bottom of the ladder and the metropolitan bourgeoisie at the top must simultaneously be exploited by the class above it (its metropolis) and exploit the class below it (its satellite). Presumably, in this scheme of things, only the classes right at the bottom of the ladder will have revolutionary potential. Poverty and exploitation become synonyms and the relatively well-off work-ing class ought to be politically conservative or reactionary.

As this book has tried to argue, such purely structural analyses may provide a starting point for discussion but are, in themselves, inadequate. Moreover, even from a purely structural point of view, this notion of a single pyramid of exploitation, oppression and poverty is a pathetic oversimplification.

7

Rural Social Structure

In a century which has become acutely conscious of the phenomenon of peasant rebellion, it sometimes comes as a surprise that Marx and many classical Marxists viewed the peasantry as a conservative force in politics. In his analysis of Bonapartism in France, Marx argued that the individualism of the petty-proprietor peasantry prevented it from coalescing as a class with a clear class consciousness. Just as potatoes in a sack would always be nothing more than a sack of potatoes, the individual form of production would keep the peasants isolated from one another and would predispose them to follow authoritarian leaders such as Bonaparte (Marx, 1967).

Some contemporary anthropologists have lent support to this notion of a conservative peasantry. In his study of Southern Italian peasants, Banfield claimed that peasant social structure was pervaded by a form of 'amoral familism', a belief that one's only loyalty was to the family, and a total distrust of anyone outside the family (Banfield, 1958). A similar conclusion was drawn by George Foster in his study of the peasants of Zintzuntzan in Mexico. They behaved, he claimed, as though their conduct was governed by an 'image of limited good'. That is, the peasants believed that the sum total of happiness, good fortune, wealth, health, etc. available to the villagers was fixed. Any increase in some kind of good to someone, therefore, was bound to be complemented by a corresponding loss elsewhere. The consequence of both amoral familism and the image of the limited good was an atmosphere of hostility and distrust, and a total inability to work together in a co-operative manner (Foster, 1967).

Yet, against this dismal picture of the egocentric and reactionary peasant, other analysts have stressed the fact of peasant participation in the great revolutions of the twentieth century. Some, following certain strains in Maoist thought, have argued that the peasantry has displaced the proletariat as the revolutionary vanguard (Caldwell, 1969).

In an excellent book, Eric Wolf analyses six major revolutions or independence struggles which have occurred in the twentieth century: the Mexican Revolution (1910–17), the Russian Revolution (1917), the Chinese Revolution (1927–49), the Cuban Revolution (1959), and the independence struggles in Algeria (1961) and Vietnam (1945–75). Describing these as 'peasant wars' Wolf attempts to explain their causes and to identify the types of peasantry which take the lead (Wolf, 1969). However, before examining Wolf's analysis in detail, one must first ask, in what sense are these events all 'peasant wars' or 'peasant revolutions'?

The Mexican Revolution began, and ended, as a bourgeois revolution against a modernising dictatorship. The peasantry, under Zapata and Villa, was not mobilised during the first stage of the revolution under Madero. Only when Madero was assassinated by the reactionary Huerta and after one of Madero's followers, Venustiano Carranza, took to the field against Huerta, were large peasant armies mobilised. Later, with the split in the revolutionary forces between the Constitutionalists and the Conventionalists, the bourgeois armies turned against the peasant armies of Villa and Zapata and smashed them. Out of the revolution came the agrarian reform, benefiting many peasants, but, after decades of persistent violence and sporadic rebellion, the new state, answerable to urban interests, finally dominated and subdued the peasantry. Some of the causes of the Mexican Revolution may have been agrarian, and in the course of the revolution the peasantry may have been mobilised as never before, but it was in its innermost nature not a peasant revolution but a bourgeois revolution.

In Russia, the insurrection was led by a party of the urban proletariat in the midst of a disintegration of the Army. The peasants in uniform, having brought about the collapse of Tsarism, returned to their villages in the expectation that the Bolsheviks would implement their programme of land, peace and bread. But from the very first days of the revolution, the Bolsheviks found themselves in a virtual civil war with the peasantry in an attempt to divert resources from the countryside to the city. That conflict lasted (like the Mexican one) until the Second World War.

China was a rather different case. After 1927, the leadership of the Communist Party formed a mass peasant army and began a process of land reform. Nevertheless, despite the importance of its agrarian programme, the Communist Party retained its non-peasant leadership and continued to dominate the peasantry through the twin apparatuses of the Communist Party and the Army. The case of Vietnam was basically similar. China and Vietnam have the strongest claim to the title of 'peasant war'.

The Algerian liberation struggle was primarily urban. It is difficult to see why this should be regarded as a peasant war, in any sense. Nor did the peasantry seriously participate in the Cuban insurrection of 1959. The Cuban peasantry has always been quite small in numbers. The bulk of the rural population is not a peasantry as such, but rather a wage-earning rural proletariat working on the sugar plantations. The leadership of the revolution, and the core of the guerilla units, was without doubt middle class, both in terms of social origin and in terms of ideological aspirations. Those peasants that joined the guerillas did so as individuals, not as a class, and the total number of combatants in the Rebel Army was always, in any case, small.

It is true that the base of operations of the Rebel Army was in the densely peasant area in the tobacco-growing provinces of the Oriente. But this location was chosen as a base of military operations primarily because of its mountainous terrain. The guerillas did not rely on the rural population for essential supplies – these came from the cities. Moreover, it is probable that the official historiography of the Cuban Revolution has understated the role played by the urban sectors in the revolt. The July 26 movement itself began as an urban insurrectionary group, and even after it had switched to rural operations, other important foci of urban opposition continued to operate. These have been pushed out of the limelight by official historiography. Only the winners are remembered.

All six revolutions raised the demand for land, but they also raised other demands, benefiting other social classes; one cannot simply isolate – without good reason – a single demand and claim that this is sufficient to describe the revolution as 'peasant'. All six revolutions carried out major land reforms, but this is hardly a satisfactory criterion, since major land reforms have been implemented under non-revolutionary governments. And in all six revolutions peasants have participated – in varying degrees – in the actual fighting. But to use this as a criterion would be akin to saying that the First and Second World Wars were 'proletarian wars' because the armies were composed primarily of workers! Crucial here is the question of organisation and leadership.

Unlike earlier peasant rebellions the organisational structures and leadership of these twentieth-century revolutions were imposed on the peasantry from outside. When analysing the class character of a revolution, it is important to consider not only the participants and the beneficiaries but also the programme and the leadership, as this will have much to do with the new form of society established after the conquest of state power. In no case can a plausible argument be put forward to the effect that the peasantry, as a class, gained control over state power. State power is always exercised by urban groups.

Indeed, the concept of 'peasant revolution' is misleading, focusing as it does on the participants rather than on the outcome of a revolution. The real issue concerns the restructuring of society and the establishment of a new hegemonic class. The peasantry, unlike the bourgeoisie or the proletariat, is not a potentially historic class; it has no hegemonic mission and its vision of society is limited to a reproduction of peasant social structure. As a consequence, peasants are always victims; they have parochial reactions to major social changes and there is always an unpredictable relationship between means and ends in peasant political action. Peasant response to challenge may vary from conservative apathy to sporadic outbursts of millenarianism and anarchic violence.

Moreover, many peasantries experience difficulty in forming a coherent class vision of their place in the social structure and have great difficulty understanding the role of social forces in the wider society. The consequence is an inability to assess accurately the likelihood of repressive action on the part of the state and hence, the occurrence of foredoomed and pathetic challenges to an implacable and merciless state. That is not to say that the peasants' view of the world is irrational, only that it is limited and therefore, in crucial aspects, distorted. James Scott has pointed out how peasants have a clear notion of their role in a moral community and how, if the moral obligations of their overlords are not fulfilled, there will be some form of response (Scott, 1976).

Nevertheless, the inability of the peasantry to play a hegemonic role in the restructuring of the social order means that we should abandon the notion of 'peasant revolution' in favour of the more precise concept of 'revolution in an agrarian society'. The task then remains of specifying the nature of the class alliances in such a revolution.

Up to now, we have talked about *the* peasantry as if it were a single homogenous whole, identical in every society. Clearly this is not so, and most (but by no means all) analysts have acknowledged this. Alavi, Moore and Wolf, for example, are concerned to discover which stratum of the peasantry plays the vanguard role in a revolution. Is it the rich peasantry, the medium peasantry, the poor peasantry or the landless peasants (Alavi, 1965; Moore, 1966; Wolf, 1969)? The evidence marshalled by the various theorists is, however, not entirely conclusive and is to some extent contradictory. There is a good reason why this should be so.

It is certainly an advance to include in the analysis some notion of the internal differentiation of the peasantry. But to assume that one single set of categories – rich, medium, poor and landless peasants – adequately fits all agrarian systems is altogether too sanguine. It is a mechanical application of ahistorical categories to quite distinct historical situations. The peasantry in India and the peasantry in Guatemala are quite different categories, just as the highland peasant in Peru is quite different from the workers in the coastal sugar plantations.

To assume that there is some single and universal category of 'peasant', 'peasant society' or 'peasant mode of production' is clearly inadequate. The peasantry is not a class; it is a conceptual category, similar to that of 'urban subordinate classes'. Just as there are different types of urban systems, so there are different types of agrarian system. Each agrarian system will specify a distinct set of rural social classes.

Incidentally, once the notion of a plurality of agrarian systems is accepted, the Byzantine debates about the correct definition of a 'peasant' become irrelevant. Peasants are henceforth defined within each agrarian system; there is no longer any universal substantive definition of a peasant. The first task of any theory of peasant politics, therefore, is the construction of a typology of agrarian systems. (I am using the phrase 'agrarian system' as though I were talking about 'agrarian modes of production', but I refrain from using the concept 'mode of production' because

it is not always the case that systems of political domination correspond to particular agrarian systems. They may do so, but there
is no necessary reason for this to happen. Therefore, in accord
with the usage of the term 'mode of production' outlined in previous
chapters, I refrain from talking about agrarian modes of production
and instead use the imprecise phrase 'agrarian system'.)

For each agrarian system we can then specify: (a) the conditions
for the political mobilisation of one or more rural classes; (b)
the circumstances leading to political conflict; and (c) the likely
outcome in terms of the kind of political movement which is likely
to be produced.

Jeffrey Paige has, to date, provided the most explicit work of
this type (Paige, 1975). Although he confines his analysis to export
agriculture, he identifies five agrarian systems.

1. The commercial manor or hacienda. An individually-owned
   enterprise which lacks power-driven processing machinery, and
   is worked by usufructuaries, resident wage labourers, or wage
   labourers who commute daily from nearby subsistence plots.
2. The sharecropped estate. An individually-owned enterprise
   which lacks power-driven processing machinery and is worked
   by sharecroppers or share-tenants. (Paige divides this type into
   centralised and decentralised sharecropping systems.)
3. The migratory labour estate. An individually-owned enterprise
   which lacks power-driven processing machinery and is worked
   by seasonal, migratory wage labourers.
4. The plantation. An enterprise owned either by a commercial
   corporation or government body, or by an individual if the
   enterprise includes power-driven processing machinery, and
   worked by wage labourers resident for continuous terms of more
   than one year.
5. The family smallholding. An individually-owned enterprise
   worked by the owner and his family.

The structural conditions making for a determinate political
response in the centralised sharecropping system are basically identical to those in the hacienda system, and the two systems may
be treated together as far as patterns of political action are concerned. According to Paige the kinds of political movements which
may be expected to occur in each of the types are as follows:

hacienda – agrarian revolt, followed by conservatism; plantation – reformist labour movement; smallholding – commodity reform movement; migratory labour estate – revolutionary nationalist movement; decentralised sharecropping – revolutionary socialist movement.

These agrarian systems do not inevitably and automatically generate the kinds of political response mentioned. In many cases there may be no significant political response at all. Other factors are required to provide the sufficient conditions for the political responses predicted by the theory. For example, in the case of the migratory labour estate, the presence of a colonial occupying power and the ability of the peasant community to provide indigenous leadership are both necessary conditions for the development of a revolutionary nationalist movement. In the case of hacienda systems, the presence of a reformist political party is one of the necessary conditions for an agrarian revolt aimed at occupation of hacienda lands.

Paige's central propositions are that:

1. Protest will only occur when there is a zero-sum conflict of interest between workers and owners. This will occur when owners cannot increase productivity except at the expense of the workers (hacienda, sharecropping, migratory labour estate systems).
2. Protest will only occur when organisational facilities are available to the workers. (Hacienda systems when there is a reformist government, migratory estates when there is colonialism and community leadership, decentralised sharecropping systems.)
3. The types of protest and the aims of the movement will be a function of the type of agrarian structure.

A summary, and gross simplification, of Paige's principal conclusions is presented in Table 4. Paige's focus on export agriculture is a salutory reminder that the underlying force behind contemporary peasant revolt is the expansion of capitalism. This is the fundamental cause singled out both by Eric Wolf and by Barrington Moore.

Wolf argues that the penetration of 'North Atlantic Capitalism' leads to population pressure, a decline in traditional authority and an ecological crisis, all of which stimulate peasant revolt.

TABLE 4   *Agrarian systems and peasant revolt*

Agrarian system	Conditions for mobilisation	Zero-sum conflict likely	Outcome
Hacienda	Reformist national government; or presence of party	Always	Peasant revolt
Plantation	Always present	Low capitalisation; lack of market control; tied labour	Reform labour movement *or* revolutionary socialist movement
Decentralised sharecropping	Absence of landlord control over local community; absence of individual mobility	Always	Revolutionary socialist movement
Migratory labour estate	Identifiable colonial enemy; community leadership	Encroachment on community lands; draining of community labour force	Revolutionary nationalist movement

SOURCE   Adapted from Paige (1975).

Unfortunately, these factors leading to peasant revolt are posed at too general a level. One can think of many instances in which there has been extensive penetration of capitalism and yet there has been no peasant revolt.

Moore refers to the process of the penetration of capitalism as the 'commercialisation of agriculture'. He argues that it breaks down a traditional balance of rights and obligations which had previously existed between landlord and peasant and that, so long as the transition from peasant to rural proletariat is *incomplete*, the peasant's perceived sense of injustice will predispose him to revolt. Peasant revolt, for Moore, is a phenomenon of the transition.

One may take exception to the implicit picture of an harmonious village community in traditional society conjured up by Moore. Reality was almost certainly quite different. Rodney Hilton has shown, in his research on the English peasantry in the Middle Ages, how there was a constant struggle between landlord and peasant over the conditions of labour. When demographic factors (for example, the Black Death) altered the balance of power in favour of the peasants (labour shortages) they tended to increase their demands and, if necessary, back them up by riot and rebellion (Hilton, 1973).

Nevertheless, as propositions about the general structural conditions leading to peasant revolt, the analyses of Wolf and Moore are useful. They need, however, to be supplemented by an analysis of the conjunctural situations, the propitious circumstances, which trigger off the revolt. For example, in hacienda systems, two conditions are necessary for revolt: (a) the presence of 'outside agitators' who can bring organisational capacity to the peasants; and (b) the existence of a reformist government to ensure that the state does not repress the peasant movement.

What these conjunctural catalysts will be, will vary from one agrarian system to another. An exhaustive and comprehensive theory of peasant politics remains to be written. All I can do here is suggest the lines that it might take and the methodological considerations it must take into account.

Even when elaborated, such a theory will apply only to ideal types. The situation in the real world will necessarily be more complex. Moreover, a theory of peasant politics must be more general in scope than a theory of peasant revolt. Agrarian politics are not simply a catalogue of continuous revolt, even though that may be true for certain periods in certain countries. Nor may the theory be static and purely typological. It must be inserted within a theory of agrarian change.

The penetration of capitalism in agriculture is not a simple process; it may take distinct forms. Lenin contrasted two such forms of agrarian development: the Junker path and the American or Kulak path. In the Junker path the landlords increase their control over the estate, to the detriment of the farm labourers, who are proletarianised. In the Kulak path, the internal differentiation of the peasantry proceeds in such a way as to enrich some peasants and impoverish others. Gradually, the rich peasants transform themselves into capitalist farmers and hire the poor peasants, now transformed into a landless rural proletariat.

As a first approximation, these two alternative paths would seem to map out the general developmental paths open to agriculture. However, just as there are a large number of different agrarian systems, and a number of different developmental paths open to distinct societies, it seems reasonable to suppose that the American and Prussian paths do not exhaust the possible forms of agricultural development. Moreover, even if we were to retain this dichotomous model of agrarian change, the two paths might be combined in a number of ways. The agrarian history of Chile provides a useful example.

By the middle of the nineteenth century, the land tenure system introduced by the Spanish settlers had evolved into a fairly stable hacienda system. A small landowning oligarchy held vast areas of land in huge haciendas. The labour force of these haciendas was partly derived from *peones* and part of the land was rented out to *inquilinos* (tenant farmers). The gold rush in Australia and California, together with a severe earthquake in Peru, opened up extensive markets for wheat in the second half of the nineteenth century. The hacienda owners of Chile responded by increasing their exports of wheat. To ensure that the maximum benefits went to the landowners, they increasingly required that the *inquilino* provide free labour for the hacienda. The *inquilino* might work himself, or he might send one or two day labourers (*peones obligados*) at his own expense. In this way, the impact of capitalism, in a situation of relative scarcity of labour, resulted in the increasingly repressive controls over labour characteristic of the Junker path (Bauer, 1975).

This system lasted until the middle of the twentieth century, even after the export markets had vanished and Chilean agriculture had lapsed into stagnation. In the 1930s, the onset of import-substitution industrialisation precipitated – through a complex series of mechanisms, including a shift in the terms of trade between agriculture and industry which was to agriculture's disadvantage – a series of changes in Chilean agriculture.

Some haciendas were subdivided and, on some of these smaller *fundos*, there was a slow shift towards more capital-intensive agriculture. The amount of land given to the *inquilinos* was reduced and the *inquilinos* were sometimes remunerated partly in money wages. Other haciendas continued, however, to produce inefficiently with traditional techniques (Kay, 1977).

In the years immediately following the Cuban Revolution of

1959, the United States launched the Alliance for Progress, designed to forestall a repetition of the Cuban insurrection elsewhere in Latin America, by a series of timely reforms which would remove the support for a revolution. Since it was widely (but incorrectly) believed that the Cuban uprising had succeeded largely due to its peasant support, agrarian reform was one of the central planks of the Alliance for Progress.

As mentioned in Chapter 4, in addition to its role in deflecting a supposedly land-hungry peasantry from revolution, land reform was seen as a cornerstone of the ECLA proposals for economic growth via income redistribution. It was expected that there might be (1) an initial drop in agricultural production as a result of organisational changes and the need for the peasants to learn to run the new co-operative farms, and (2) a reduction in the amount of foodstuffs marketed, as the peasantry increased their own consumption levels. Nevertheless, the ECLA economists assumed that this would be a passing phase, followed by expanding agricultural production and increased consumption of domestically-manufactured goods by the beneficiaries of the reform. (The evidence to support this analysis is somewhat controversial. There are many technical aspects to agrarian reform programmes which cannot be dealt with here for the lack of space but which affect the outcome of a reform programme.)

At any rate, the general assumption was that, in the first place, the peasantry would be satisfied with the new access to land and would become a conservative bulwark for the regime. In addition, the reform would trigger off a process of internal differentiation within the peasantry, and the emerging Kulak stratum would further consolidate bourgeois hegemony in the countryside.

Chile, with its mass working-class parties, and its traditional and inefficient haciendas, was a prime candidate for Alliance for Progress reforms. By the 1960s the costs of maintaining such an inefficient agriculture were becoming politically too high for the expanding urban population and a series of land reform laws were passed. The intention was to expropriate the large, inefficient haciendas and hand them over, either as co-operatives or as small-holdings, to the *inquilinos*. The long-term result of this reform would be the emergence of the American path toward capitalism in agriculture.

Simultaneously with this trend emerged a counter-trend. The

1960s saw, in addition to the agrarian reform, a rapid development of rural unions. The effect of the unionisation process was twofold. On the one hand, it further accelerated the process of proletarianisation which had begun in the 1930s, when the conservative symbiosis of hacienda and *inquilino* began to dissolve. On the other hand, in an inflationary situation, the rural unions increasingly demanded more land, thus pushing the system back towards one of labour-service tenantry.

Thus, over the course of a century, Chilean agriculture had embarked on the Junker path, only to get stuck in an unproductive and stagnant equilibrium between 1880 and 1930. The industrialisation process of the 1930s began to disturb this equilibrium and generated a profound crisis in Chilean agriculture. The responses to this crisis were complex and contradictory, but generally seemed to favour the American path. This trend seems to have become the dominant one with the application of the agrarian reform of the 1960s and 1970s.

Throughout this period, the Chilean peasantry remained locked in to the hacienda, more or less insulated from the process of political radicalisation occurring in the urban centres throughout the twentieth century. Until the land reform and unionisation of the 1960s, the landowners had been able to persuade the middle-class parties which exercised control over much of the state apparatus to prevent the incursion of leftist political organisers inside the haciendas. The changing class alliances of the 1960s destroyed this hands-off pact, and the peasantry changed overnight from a passive and inert mass, accustomed to voting at the direction of their *patrón*, to a radical and destabilising force. The change, of course, was not due to some mysterious inner change in the peasants, but to the lifting of the coercive sanctions which had encapsulated the peasantry within the hacienda system..

The return to the American path required the successful completion of a series of technical innovations in agriculture if productivity was to be raised. Otherwise this path would lead, not to capitalist agriculture, but to stagnation and rural misery. Many anthropological studies indicate that the presence of market opportunities is not in itself sufficient to induce peasants to adopt new crops or new technologies which would increase their income and, simultaneously, greatly raise agricultural productivity.

For decades, particularly with the advent of the 'green revolution',

rural sociologists grappled with the problem of peasant resistance
to innovation. This manifestation of peasant conservatism threatened to destroy the viability of the American road to capitalism,
and leave the field open to the great landlords to follow the Prussian
path. In the aftermath of the Cuban Revolution, this path was
generally felt to bring with it the spectre of peasant revolution.
Consequently, land reform and increases in agricultural productivity
had to go hand-in-hand.

In general, it seems that the slow rate of diffusion of innovations
was due, not to ignorance or conservatism, but rather to the high
element of risk attached. At levels of production close to subsistence,
the adoption of an innovation – if it failed – incurred the real
risk of starvation. Hence, only relatively well-off peasants were
in a position to innovate.

In this situation, and in the absence of some form of insurance
against crop failure, the introduction of high-yield varieties of rice
and wheat, or of machinery, tended to increase rural stratification.
The richer farmers adopted the new seeds or machinery and increased their profits. In turn, their increased profits enabled them
to expand their holdings at the expense of the poorer peasants
who were increasingly proletarianised (Griffin, 1974). In addition,
the introduction of high-yield varieties and the construction of
irrigation systems frequently set in motion a series of ecological
changes which further intensified the risk factor in peasant agriculture.

The upshot of the 'green revolution' has been the introduction,
or the exacerbation, of a dualism in agriculture between the Junker
path and the American path. All too often, as in Mexico for
example, the effect of agrarian reform has been to give an impulse
to the large, technically efficient modern sector and to retain the
mass of the population as reserve labour force, trapped on their
tiny and unproductive parcels of land (Bartra, 1975). This poverty-
stricken, semi-proletarianised peasantry can remain politically quiescent for decades, sometimes supporting authoritarian regimes, sometimes giving way to millennial despair or, more pragmatically, banditry. But when inserted in an auspicious structure of class alliances,
this smouldering discontent can be ignited overnight.

A similar dynamic explains the waves of peasant protest in Brazil.
Until the 1880s, Brazil could be characterised as a form of rural
patrimonialism. A weak central state effectively devolved power

to local agrarian oligarchies. Each *fazendero* (estate owner) retained
his own private militia and was responsible for the maintenance
of law and order within his domain. When conflicts occurred
between *fazenderos*, kin feuds arose, and settled the power of the
various dynastic groups. Under this system, the Brazilian peasantry
remained quiescent and subordinate to the *fazenderos*.

However, in the period between 1870 and 1930, this system
began to break down. The central state began to increase its
power, and with the growth of coffee in the Centre–South of the
country, the established agrarian oligarchies of the North-east began
to decay. The disintegration of the patrimonial political system
was accompanied by a form of political banditry known as the
cangaço. The severe drought of 1877 and the ensuing economic
collapse and mass labour migration was one of the factors precipitat-
ing the collapse of the system. Only after the realignment of political
alliances in the 1930s were the *cangacieros* suppressed and tranquility
restored to the North-east (de Souza, 1972).

Banditry is a common form of peasant protest in situations where
a class alliance with some urban force capable of restructuring
agriculture is not feasible. When such an alliance is not an option,
peasant protest may take several forms (messianism, anarchic uprisings, tax evasion, etc.) of which banditry may be one. The *cangaço*
seems to have had this character. However, it should be borne
in mind that not all forms of banditry are forms of peasant revolt.
Anton Blok's study of the Sicilian mafia suggests that it was not
so much an authentic form of peasant protest as an informal repressive apparatus which mediated between the central Italian state
and the feudal landowners of Sicily. As such, the mafia acquired
a great deal of autonomy and was able to use terror to produce
its own pecuniary reward (Blok, 1974). Moreover, many forms of
peasant protest, of which banditry is one, can only thrive when
the central state apparatus cannot or does not effectively control
rural areas. This may stem directly from a weakness of the central
state apparatus, or may be a result of a stalemated conflict between
the central state and the various rural power-holders. Such situations
of class balance tend not to last very long, and with the establishment
of the hegemony of one or other of the contending parties, the
'rural problem' is likely to be 'solved'.

In 1930 Getúlio Vargas became president of Brazil and in 1934
set about the construction of the *Estado Nôvo*, the new state. The

Estado Nôvo saw the transfer of hegemony to the coffee growers and the industrialists of São Paulo. The North-eastern oligarchies were reintegrated into the alliance in a subordinate status, later formalised in a new political party, the PSD. The dominance of the landowners in the rural areas was to be absolute. Where necessary the state would intervene to establish order. With the consolidation of the new class alliance, the *cangaço* was repressed.

Rural unrest did not flare up again until the class alliances set up by the *Estado Nôvo* began to fall apart in the 1950s. The reformist and populist governments of Kubitscheck and Goulart (1956−64) were confronted with the imminent demise of the ISI growth model. Their response, particularly that of Goulart, was to strengthen the class alliance on its left wing. The radical-populist elements of the coalition, and the trade unions, began to have increasing weight within the class alliance. As government policy moved towards the left, and as the NCOs in the army and navy looked as if they would support Goulart against a possible military intervention, the bourgeoisie and landed oligarchy pulled away from the alliance, forcing Goulart to rely even more heavily on the popular sectors.

This slow disintegration of the political alignments of the *Estado Nôvo* was the setting for the rapid rise of the peasant leagues in the North-east under the leadership of Fransisco Juliâo. While Juliâo organised the renters and sharecroppers of the semi-arid *sertão*, the Communist Party and the Catholic Church both set out to organise the sugar workers on the coastal plantations. In the end, the potential threat posed by this wave of rural organisation was conjured away by the military *coup* of 1964. The reorganisation of the development project under the aegis of the military, with its reassertion of the unity of purpose of the state, meant the suppression of the peasant leagues.

What can be seen from the examples of Chile and Brazil is that the peasantry will remain passive (or turn to millennialism and other apolitical forms of action) so long as the hegemony of the rural oligarchy is unchallenged. When a structural shift in the economic growth model brings about a disintegration of the dominant class alliance, the peasantry will almost certainly engage in massive political or quasi-political revolt. Only with the recomposition of a new dominant class alliance and the re-establishment of a new development project will the state be able to restore 'order' to the rural zones.

In this sense, the emphasis laid by Wolf and Moore on the

declining authority of rural elites following the penetration of capitalism in agriculture is correct. However, the site of that degeneration of authority is to be sought primarily in the state apparatus and in the class alliance supporting that state. One can only move from changing economic structures in agriculture to peasant politics via an analysis of class alliances at the level of the state apparatus. Other forms of analysis can only be partial explanations, to be inserted into the larger picture.

8

Politics, the State, the Military

The principal hypothesis in this chapter is that, to each of the forms of economic development there corresponds a particular form of politics and form of state apparatus. Of course, this can only be hypothesised in the most general terms, since we have stressed the importance of the class structure in mediating between the economy and the polity.

In Latin America, the export economies had as their political correlate a system of oligarchical politics, in which the rural elites directly controlled the nation-state and in which other social classes were excluded from power. In some countries, this oligarchical rule was achieved through a strong and centralised state apparatus, as in Chile, though this tended to be the exception. In many countries, the local landowning families tended to establish political fiefs and the national state apparatus interfered little in local affairs. In these circumstances, the national state became principally an arena for infighting over the distribution of patronage and revenue. Which form of state occurred was to a great degree a function of the degree of integration of the landowning class. As we noted in Chapter 6, this was in turn a consequence of the way in which the export economy was integrated into the world system. Brazil and Chile provide clear examples. In Chile the mining operations in the northern deserts were controlled by foreign corporations and the landowners of the central valley formed a cohesive and homogenous class which used the state apparatus to extract revenues from the mining companies and use them for their own benefit. In Brazil, on the other hand, the agricultural exporting operations were almost always domestically owned.

Brazil's exports changed considerably over the course of the nine-teenth and twentieth centuries and the regions where the various products (coffee, cacao, sugar, rubber, etc.) were grown, shifted, with the consequence that a series of local elites sprang into existence and maintained themselves as quite distinct fractions of the dominant class. The end result was a form of patrimonial politics in which there was considerable local autonomy and in which the national state was relatively weak *vis-à-vis* the local landed interests.

The beginning of the twentieth century saw the emergence of new social classes, the urban middle class and the nascent proletar-iat, and the beginning of their attempts to gain political power. The world depression of the 1930s brought about an immediate crisis of the oligarchical states and presented these new power contenders with the opportunity to displace the oligarchy. In the 1930s, the political movements of this nature took the form of populism in many countries, though there were, of course, consider-able local variations.

Populism appears, in fact, not simply as the form of politics assumed by the Latin American societies during the great depression but as the generic form of politics in the Third World. Underlying the apparently heterogeneous political movements of the Third World, some observers claim to have discerned an underlying simi-larity in the predominance of populism. The political movements of the Third World are seen as populist movements, and the task of the investigator is then to explain the common causative elements which produce populist responses in so many apparently diverse situations (Ionescu and Gellner, 1969).

Populism as a political movement is not organised along class lines. This is perhaps its defining feature. It operates with a theoreti-cal framework in which the people or the nation are opposed to the anti-nation, usually concretely identified as a foreign power, or their domestic servants or an oligarchy which is deemed to hold back the progress of the nation. Populism denies that society is divided along class lines, and in its diffuse, inchoate and contradic-tory ideology, it asserts that the only important political division is between the people and their enemies, internal and external (Harris, 1968). Populist movements are usually not organised as parties but as loose movements of a leader and his following (the relevance of Weber's analysis of charisma is obvious here).

Analysts of populist movements have often concurred with the populists themselves and asserted that populist movements are indeed not organised along class lines. The theorists of mass society, in a kind of analysis very close to their discussions of the phenomenon of marginality, argue that it is the marginal mass and recent immigrants who provide the human basis for populist movements. I have argued in Chapter 6 that such approaches are probably mistaken in their analysis of the nature of class formation in the Third World. The supporters of populist movements are not a marginal mass but part of social classes in the process of formation. Other analysts, in the tradition of marginality analysis, have asserted that, while the populists do not constitute a marginal mass, they are from groups or sectors which in some sense are 'outside' modern class society, and represent a reaction against it. The populists are the rural reactionaries, in the countryside or in the city.

If we accept this ideal-type description of populism initially, then we can see that the key defining feature of populism is, in fact, its ideology. Movements are described as populist or not according to whether certain ideological traits can be shown to be present. On this basis, the assumption seems to be made that one can therefore define a single political phenomenon which will have a unique set of causes. This may be the case, but methodological considerations would suggest that it is not likely to be a profitable way to proceed.

Normally, if one were to set up a chain of causation and search for regularities in political behaviour, one would begin with an analysis of a structural situation which would have a propensity to give rise to a certain kind of movement. One would then go on to consider the forces which influenced the ideological statements of that movement. The chain of causation and explanation would go from structural situations to social movement to ideology. The methodology applied by many analysts of populism seems to be exactly the reverse of this. Consequently, it is highly likely that strange conclusions will be arrived at. Similar ideological themes may well mask quite diverse interests and embody distinct class projects. Ideologies are very flexible and populism is merely one *strand* in an overall ideological framework. Similar ideologies do not necessarily indicate that the movements which have produced them, or the structural situations that have produced the movements, have anything in common. They may, but this is not a very reliable methodological assumption.

The analysts of populism often fall into another, rather elementary mistake. That is to assume that because a movement claims to be classless, that it is indeed classless. However, a movement which claims to be classless may well be composed of classes or at least identifiable in terms of classes and class interests.

To see what this might mean, let us look more closely at some specific populist movements in Latin America. In general, populism represented a response to the crisis brought about by the great depression. It was not simply a response to problems of modernisation, nor simply a phenomenon of transition, nor was it simply a movement of groups and societies which are peripheral to the centres of power. All these may well have been aspects of the phenomenon, but these explanations are couched in terms too general to be of much use. Populism was a response to a specific historical situation, the collapse of the export-oriented growth model, and the attendant crisis of the oligarchic state.

The response of the power holders to the crisis of the 1930s was either a set of policies which, whether intentionally or not, promoted ISI (this usually happened only in the more industrially advanced countries of the region) or increased repression to deal with popular discontent. This happened in the smaller countries as a rule.

Where ISI was embarked on, this required a restructuring of class relations around a new development project. Hegemony had to shift from the oligarchy to the new industrial bourgeoisie or to elites acting on its behalf, and the political system and the state apparatus had to be reorganised. To achieve this, the bourgeoisie sought allies in the working class and urban middle class. To a large measure their real interests coincided, though always only partially. Populism was the ideology which cemented this class alliance and expressed the common interests of the various classes. However, partly because the bourgeoisie and the .working class were still new social classes and still not fully cognisant of their interests and oppositions, and partly because the coincidence of interests was only partial, some form of ideology (in the sense of obfuscation of real conflicts) was necessary. In these terms, populism was indeed a transitional political form, since one could expect bourgeois hegemony to be established and the populist elements of the class alliance to drop away.

One should not always emphasise the 'newness' of the working class. Some writers have suggested that only a proletariat of recent formation, fresh from the countryside, still an unorganised mass, is susceptible to populist appeals. In this form of analysis, populism is less a form of class alliance than a form of charismatic manipulation of masses by elites.

This may correspond to the situation in some countries. In Argentina, however, the evidence does not support this interpretation. Working-class support for Perón came as much from the older, established trade unions as from the newer sectors of the working class (Little, 1975; Murmis and Portantiero, 1971). In fact, the dependent nature of the Third World countries makes the achievement of any kind of stable hegemony extremely problematic, and hence makes the possibility of forms of populist challenge a perennial one. This, in general terms, would seem to be what happened in Latin America as a whole. The process, of course, took different forms in different countries.

It was not, of course, always the case that the bourgeoisie as a whole challenged the oligarchy as a whole. As we have seen, in Chile the amalgamation of bourgeoisie and oligarchy into a single class prevented the emergence of populism. Instead, we find a relatively unified upper class challenged by the middle class and the working class. The result was a system of compromises and permanent negotiation–incorporation in the form of a bourgeois parliamentary democracy (Zeitlin, 1968).

Nor did a unified bourgeoisie challenge a unified oligarchy in Peronist Argentina, often held to be a classic example of populism. The situation was quite the opposite of Chile. According to Murmis and Portantiero (1971), both the bourgeoisie and the agrarian oligarchy were deeply divided internally. The agrarian oligarchy was split into the breeders, who raised cattle in the Southern region, and the fatteners, who bought the cattle from the breeders and pastured them in the rich lands near Buenos Aires before selling them to the big slaughtering and freezing firms.

For its part the bourgeoisie was split between the *Union Industrial* (UI), which organised the monopoly sectors associated with the export trade, and the *Confederación General de Empresarios* (CGE), which was composed of smaller industrialists who stood to gain from the ISI policies adopted by Perón.

In the end, the CGE and the fatteners supplied the upper-class elements of the Peronist coalition, while the UI and the breeders remained in opposition. Bonapartism in Argentina, and its populist support, thus expressed not simply an equilibrium between an oligarchy and a bourgeoisie, but a more complicated situation in which each of the dominant classes was itself profoundly divided.

Once the oligarchies had been displaced from the centre of power by the new populist alliance, the tasks facing the emerging bourgeoisie were twofold. On the one hand, it was imperative to ensure that, within the bounds of its own class alliance, the bourgeoisie was the dominant partner in the coalition. On the other hand, and growing out of this first requirement for domination, the bourgeoisie increasingly found it imperative to increase its freedom of action *vis-à-vis* its erstwhile allies. The bourgeoisie could not indefinitely satisfy the demands of a mobilised working class, and if capital accumulation was to proceed without major problems, some way had to be found to displace the working class from power and institutionalise it in a subordinate position. Yet this subordination and exclusion of the working class had to be carried out in such a way as to prevent a violent class conflict which might imperil the fragile political stability enjoyed by the new regime.

Simultaneously, since the old oligarchies had merely been displaced, and not destroyed, some form of reaccommodation with them was indispensable. At this point, the bourgeoisie appears to have moved to the right as it searched for some kind of equilibrium between the contending social classes – which were generally much stronger than the bourgeoisie itself. The bourgeoisie attempted to increase its own autonomy, its own freedom of action with respect to the other social classes. A common result of this process was the emergence of various forms of Bonapartist dictatorship. The governments of Perón in Argentina and Getúlio Vargas in Brazil are classic examples of this form of politics. However, the balance achieved by these regimes was often precarious and achieved only at the cost of the isolation of the government from any organised social base of support. Isolated and unstable, they could be toppled with relative facility, as they stumbled from one economic and political crisis to the next.

As a solution to this situation of hyper-autonomy, the political elite at times attempted to create political institutions which were capable of providing a stable base of support for the government without allowing too much freedom of action to other classes.

It is in this attempt to create authoritative institutions that some theorists, notably Samuel Huntington, have seen the key to political 'modernisation'. In Huntington's words, 'The most important political distinction among countries concerns not their form of government, but their degree of government' (Huntington, 1968, p. 1). What has happened, according to this theory, is that the growing number of political actors has increased the number and scope of demands made on the political system. The rising expectations have led to a heightened level of conflict, which has, at the same time, become potentially more complex and difficult to resolve as the number of actors increases. Over time, conflict becomes increasingly difficult to manage. The process may be described as one in which the increase in mobilisation outstrips the process of institutionalisation. The problem of political development therefore consists in the creation of a legitimate public order, via the creation of authoritative institutions.

When political modernisation (the creation of new, authoritative institutions) is not achieved, a form of praetorian politics emerges. Praetorian politics is characterised by the absence of political institutions which can mediate group conflict and by the absence of agreement on legitimate *methods* for resolving conflicts. Power and authority become fragmented and parcelled out and the polity exists in a situation of perpetual crisis.

Despite the functionalist overtones, in its emphasis on the dual problem of mobilisation and institutionalisation, Huntington's theory focuses on the central issue of politics – the problem of order. One might well disagree with Huntington at the point where he asserts that the *content* of political order is of little interest. The implication is that there exists a single, unilinear dimension of political modernisation, measured by the adequacy of institutions to meet the challenges of mobilisation at any given time. The theory does not explore the reasons *why* mobilisation should occur at some periods, rather than others; it takes the sources of mobilisation as basically unproblematic and in so doing, tends to take on an ahistorical quality.

The formal nature of Huntington's theory thereby tends to obscure the class nature of major structural shifts in underdeveloped societies. Let us examine two major structural shifts which have occurred in some Latin American societies, the shift from export-orientation to ISI, and the shift, in the 1960s from the ISI model to the so-called 'Brazilian' model, based on the growth of multinational corporations inside the economic space of underdeveloped countries. Both transitions are similar in that there is considerable mobilisation of subordinate classes, followed by repression and a recomposition of the dominant classes around a modified and expanded state apparatus. In the formal political science terms employed by Huntington, the two situations are remarkably similar. However, if we look more closely at the actual social forces involved, there appear to be substantial differences. In the first transition, we are dealing with a new working class, weakly organised and with only limited and inappropriate anarchist traditions and forms of organisation as its political heritage. By the 1950s and 1960s, in the countries which experienced the second transition (the more industrially developed nations like Brazil and Mexico) the working class had developed a considerable degree of organisation and political experience. It was a working class frustrated by the failure of the ISI period to give it much in the way of economic benefits or access to political power. For this reason among others, the new state had to be much more repressive. The forms assumed by the state apparatuses after the second transition greatly exceeded those assumed by the Bonapartist dictatorships of the 1930s and 1940s in terms of repressive capacity.

What I have tried to argue here is that the ability to organise certain forms of class alliance is (a) partly a function of a given historical situation and (b) constrains the implementation of any specific development model. Specific forms of class alliance, organised around particular development projects, mould the kinds of political institutions (and in particular, the form of state power) which arise. The emergence of political institutions, therefore, can only be understood in relation to specific class projects.

As an example, let us consider the issue of democracy. It has been argued that there is a connection between economic growth and democracy, by which is meant adult franchise, free elections, a plurality of political parties and a set of constitutional checks and balances between the various branches of the state apparatus. (Of course, there is considerable debate about what we mean by 'democracy', but most political scientists have in mind some kind of operational definition in terms of a set of institutions and processes similar to the one given above.) According to S. M. Lipset, examination of historical data indicates a weak but positive correlation between economic development and democracy. (However, it should be pointed out that Lipset uses cross-sectional data and makes longitudinal inferences from that data, which is, on purely methodological grounds, rather suspect.) He concludes that, with advances in economic growth, there will be a correlative shift towards more democratic political systems (Lipset, 1959).

However, as the decades of the 1960s and 1970s have shown, such hopes have proved to be too sanguine, and a different perspective has tended to come to the fore. This second perspective argues that the imperatives of capital accumulation require the establishment of an *authoritarian* political regime, capable of dealing with the tensions and frustrations engendered by the economic growth process (de Schweinitz, 1964).

In sharp contrast to the ISI theorists, who believed that income redistribution and economic growth were not only compatible but also necessarily complementary, this group of theorists see a set of sharp dichotomies which face policy-makers. According to them, policy-makers must choose between distribution and accumulation in the sphere of economics. This choice implies another, second choice between building political support and implementing unpopular growth policies, and ultimately, a choice between democracy and authoritarianism (Skidmore, 1977; Malloy, 1970).

A similar analysis has been made by Marxists such as Paul Baran, who argues that even a socialist government would be faced with a similar set of dilemmas in its first years, and would have to opt for authoritarian rule in order to stimulate economic growth. A similar argument could be put forward as a partial explanation of the necessity of Stalinist forced industrialisation in the USSR (Baran, 1957).

Two comments need to be made about this style of analysis. First, if underdevelopment is largely due to the *misallocation*, rather than the absolute absence of resources, it should be possible to reallocate existing resources so as to increase the rate of growth without severe sacrifices on the part of any sector of the population. However, the degree to which such a painless move toward optimal resource allocation would be possible in any concrete situation must be historically variable.

The second and more important point once again concerns the abstract and ahistorical nature of the argument. Rather than seeing political democracy as a simple concomitant of economic growth *per se*, it seems more rewarding to examine the constellations of class conflict which give rise to specific political forms. (It should be clear that I am here talking about a political *form*; whether a government or its policies is *popular* is rather a different matter. Thus, Cuba may have an undemocratic but popular government while Colombia may be a democracy but yet not have a popular government. Democracy, as I have defined it, is government *by* the people; whether it is government *for* the people is a separate issue.)

Chile, for example, was able to maintain a healthy political democracy throughout most of the twentieth century (unlike many other Latin American nations) because of its peculiar class structure. For a start, the unified dominant class was not seriously split, as were the oligarchies and bourgeoisies of other countries. This unified dominant class was a product of Chile's development as an exporter of nitrates and copper from foreign-owned mining enclaves in the North of the country. The Chilean ruling class was able to establish its social base in the great haciendas of the Central Valley, and use the state to tax the mineral enclaves for development funds and for the running expenses of the state apparatus. This use of the state to tax the mineral enclaves was to enable a relatively painless sharing of power to occur over the course of the twentieth century as the middle classes and, later, the working class came increasingly to demand access to state power.

In a complex process of concessions, repression and occasional political upheaval, the confident and unified ruling class of Chile gradually admitted the parties of the middle and working classes into the political arena, incorporating them into the political system as brokers between the ruling class and the subordinate classes. A form of parliamentary clientelistic politics emerged in which the spoils from copper were used to support an industrialisation programme which hurt nobody. Politically, this arrangement had three key preconditions. First, the power of the landed upper class was left intact. The Radical and Popular Front governments of the 1940s explicitly accepted a 'hands-off' pact and did not attempt to organise the peasantry. Secondly, throughout the period, both the Socialist and Communist Parties, each with a mass working-class base, accepted the rules of the parliamentary game and increasingly evolved in the direction of classical social-democratic reformism.

(Though never totally, as the experience of the Allende Government was later to demonstrate.) Thirdly, the Radical Party (and later, to some extent, the Christian Democratic Party) played a central role in ensuring simultaneously the support of the middle classes for the political system and the dominance of bourgeois economic policies in government.

In other countries of the region, where the ruling classes were internally divided, and where there was no easy foreign-owned source of government revenue, the danger of allowing other social classes to organise independently and autonomously was too great to be permitted. Other forms of political institutions had to be developed. These ranged from the repression and exclusion of subordinate classes, through various forms of populist domination over those classes in the interests of fractions of the bourgeoisie, to various forms of corporate inclusion of all classes (but in a way so that they were disorganised as classes) into a single political party – such as Mexico's PRI (Partido Revolucionario Institucional, or Institutional Revolutionary Party).

It should be noted that the very premises of Chilean democracy could turn, when conditions altered, into serious threats to that very democracy. Chilean democracy depended quite directly on a steady revenue from mineral exports. When that faltered in the 1920s and 1930s, there were immediate political repercussions. The 1920s and 1930s saw a spate of military conspiracies, interventions in politics and mutinies. There were also attempts at a socialist revolution, the most notable of which was the eight-day Socialist Republic of 1932. And in 1970, the heritage of decades of parliamentary democracy was a real and powerful factor in allowing Salvador Allende to be inaugurated President. In other less democratic countries a pre-emptive veto *coup* by the military would have foreclosed such a possibility. That did not happen in Chile, and it was only when the government of the Popular Unity clearly posed a serious threat to bourgeois institutionality as such that the army stepped in. Had there not existed a real history of democracy in Chile, the class struggle could never have taken the form that it did, the only form appropriate to Chile's history.

THE STATE AND THE MILITARY

There has been, and continues to be, considerable debate (particularly within Marxist circles) about the nature of the state. The problem is, how can the state be 'relatively autonomous' from a social base in the ruling class and yet continue to serve the interests of that class?

In an attempt to answer this question a number of writers, of whom Althusser and Poulantzas are the most well-known, have suggested that the structural organisation of the state apparatus is sufficient to ensure that it acts on behalf of the dominant class. In Althusser's work, this becomes a simple functionalist tautology – the state is *defined* as that which serves to maintain the functioning of the social formation (Althusser, 1969). In other words, the state is that analytic aspect of any institution which acts to reproduce the existing social order. Hence, Althusser sees the state in such institutions as schools, the church, the family, ideology, etc. All these become, in his terminology, 'state apparatuses'. It should be obvious that such an approach is not only very similar to the functionalism of Talcott Parsons but also represents a backward step from that position. It is confusing enough to equate the state with Parsons' L-system (Parsons, 1951); it is totally retrograde to then go on to assert that this set of functions is in fact a set of apparatuses (that is, institutions) whereas it is only a set of *analytical aspects* of those institutions. At all events, the state is defined, not by what it does, but by what it is. In contrast to Althusser, I shall treat the state as a structured and interlocking set of institutions.

Poulantzas' position is ambiguous. It is not the same as Althusser's, in that in his more concrete work, he talks primarily about political institutions. By so doing, he manages to avoid Althusser's functionalist tautology and answers the question of why the state serves the interest of the dominant class in a different way. It does so, he says, because of its *structure*. Whatever the social background or personal goals of the occupants of the roles in the state apparatus, they cannot alter the nature of the state. The way in which the roles are structured *necessitates* one outcome; the maintenance of the state as a capitalist state (Poulantzas, 1973).

It could be argued against this that Poulantzas' position is pure reification. That a given structure of roles tends to persist is not an *explanation* of that persistence, nor is it any indication of how long that structure will persist. To assert that the structure of roles which comprises a state will persist because of the way in which it is structured is simply an unproven assertion.

Against Poulantzas, it seems much more reasonable to argue that there are concrete explanations for why actors fulfil certain role-expectations. (These have primarily to do either with social background or socialisation.) Consequently, under certain conditions, the incumbents of certain roles may behave in a deviant manner. This may have all sorts of consequences for the actions undertaken by the state apparatus. Unlike Althusser and Poulantzas, it seems to us that Weber was quite correct when he emphasised the *problematic* nature of state power. The state is not a thing, or an instrument, to be captured and used. Nor is it some kind of automatic society-maintaining function. It is a set of institutions. And institutions are only more or less stable patterns of interpersonal behaviour and expectations. As such, they are always potentially subject to change. Accordingly, in this chapter, I will attempt to identify some of the conditions which affect the class nature of the state.

It is generally accepted that the state in contemporary underdeveloped societies is exceptional in the sense that it is strong and authoritarian, and has a high degree of 'relative autonomy' from any social base. These terms are not always easy to define. For example, to speak of a state as 'strong' may be merely a way of saying that organised social forces are weak. The state may be strong in relation to existing social classes, but is it strong in the sense of being able effectively to establish its control throughout the national territory? That kind of strength is not often encountered in contemporary underdeveloped societies. Many 'strong' states are faced with seemingly endemic and ineradicable foci of discontent which may take the form of banditry, mafia or of rural or urban guerillas.

The concept of 'relative autonomy' is also highly problematic. This term has been given different meanings by various writers, and has come to mean a number of things. It might refer to the extent to which the political sphere is relatively autonomous from the rest of the social structure, obeying its own laws of motion, at least in the short run.

Unless one is dealing with a model of social structures in which all causal or functional relations are total, immediate and direct (so that a change in any one part of the system has immediate and determinate repercussions elsewhere), then it is always the case that the various spheres will have their own levels of 'autonomy' such that processes within any particular sphere cannot simply be reduced to effects of changes in other spheres. This problem is conceptualised in Marxist theory as the relationship between base and superstructure. I do not, of course, claim to offer any new insights into this issue; however, the position adopted in this book should be stated explicitly. It is assumed that there is a chain of causality going from the economic sphere to the social structure (including the formation of social classes) and thence to the political and cultural (ideological) systems. However, the causality, which links one level to another, may be extremely weak and, although in any explanation one will always move from the economy to politics via the social structure, one cannot simply extrapolate from changes in the economic sphere to changes in the political sphere. The chains of causality are too complex, and the causality itself is weak. The position adopted, therefore, may be classified as one of partial economic determination, rather than a rigorous economic determinism. From this point of view, there is always some relative autonomy of politics and this is therefore not a problem specific to the study of underdevelopment.

Moreover, there is a very real sense in which, when discussing underdeveloped countries, we are not dealing with a single endogenously-determined system (in which the problematic element is 'simply' the degree of systemness or closure versus the degree of autonomy of the various structural components of the system), but rather with two nested systems. The system of the nation-state is embedded in a separate and larger system, that of the world economy and the system of nation-states. As we have argued in the sections on imperialism and dependency, the way in which the countries of the periphery have been inserted into this larger world system during its historical development have profound effects on the internal functioning of the nation-states of the Third World, considered as systems.

Alternatively, relative autonomy might refer to the extent to which the state ·apparatus is independent of, or insulated from, the direct influence of the dominant classes. The state, in this second sense, would be relatively autonomous if the dominant classes did not have direct access to, or control over, the state apparatus. Clearly, this is a matter of degree. The ways in which the interests of the dominant classes are connected with the actual functioning of the state apparatus are highly variable, and are amenable to historical investigation.

One view of the relationship between ruling class and state apparatus is contained in the remarks in the Communist Manifesto to the effect that the state is the executive body of the ruling class. The implication is that members of the dominant class occupy the key positions in the state apparatus and, for this reason, the state functions as a class state, that is in the interests of the dominant class. They possess the state in the same way that they possess the means of production.

However, it is empirically observable that this model does not apply to all states. (That is not to say, on the other hand, that it does not apply to *some*.) In cases where the state apparatus is not manned by members of the ruling class, several things may be happening. It may be that the state functionaries have been socialised in such a way that they perceive the interests of the ruling class and their interests (usually expressed as the interests of the society as such) to be identical. The explanation for the functioning of the class state is therefore to be sought in the operation of a set of institutions which socialise state functionaries into the world-view of the dominant class. When those processes of socialisation fail, the state will cease to function 'automatically' as a class state.

Alternatively, the functionaries of the state apparatus may well have a different world-view from the dominant class but may nevertheless act in its interests because there is a measure of coincidence or identity of interests between the functionaries and the dominant class. This might express a form of class alliance (to the extent that the state functionaries are recruited from or embody the aspirations of a specific social class) or may simply be an alliance between the dominant class and the political elite of state functionaries (who have their own specific interests *qua* functionaries). The extent to which state functionaries are conscious of their own, or their class's interests or are rather merely the bearers of an ideology which serves the dominant class cannot be defined in advance; it is an empirical question.

Another possibility is that, in a situation in which the dominant class is internally divided and neither faction can impose its will on the other, some third force such as a military leader may occupy the state apparatus and rule on behalf of the dominant class as a whole. This is the phenomenon which Marx described as Bonapartism and which Gramsci referred to as Caesarism. There are two distinct situations in which this may occur. The first is simply a stalemate between two class fractions or between two classes. As long as this stalemate continues, there is a situation of catastrophic equilibrium within the state. (Such a catastrophic equilibrium might also occur in society as a whole as two social forces confront each other.) The second situation is one in which power is being transferred from one class or fraction to another, and a recomposition of the bloc in power is being organised. This process of reorganisation of the dominant classes may be overseen by some third force, which may even have interests of its own. Populism in Latin America in the 1930s is the classic example of this form of Bonapartism. As the industrial bourgeoisie displaced the landed oligarchy, a military leader with popular support temporarily seized control of the state. His policies lead, inevitably, to his own downfall and (though not inevitably) to the dominance of the industrial bourgeoisie within the state apparatus. At times, this transition may be blocked and the state may become the arena of political struggle as diverse social forces struggle for access to state power. Such a situation, in which the state is open and exposed to political forces and in which no single social class can impose its own developmental project on society, has been called by Huntington a situation of Praetorian politics.

In this perspective, considering the state as an instrument of power to be wielded by whichever class gains control over its institutions, one sees immediately the problematic nature of state power in many of the societies of the Third World. Clearly, in a situation in which there is no single hegemonic class, but rather a series of contending rival forces (perhaps based on the successive development of regionally-based oligarchies, as in Brazil), the state will be perceived by many social forces as a target, as the prize of political struggle. One outcome may be a Praetorian situation. Another outcome may involve a series of shifting compromises whereby power is effectively parcelled out through a reorganisation of the state apparatus. The most obvious form in which this reorganisation might occur would be a devolution of power to regional power apparatuses and a delimitation on the ability of the central state to intervene in certain kinds of local political conflicts. Another form which this disaggregation of the state apparatus might take is the penetration of local or class-specific interests in the operation of the state apparatus via a system of corruption or clientelistic politics. Here the formal rationality of the machinery of the state is subverted to the particularistic aims of those social classes that are able to use corruption or ties of kinship and influence to affect policy outputs. Incidentally, this may be one of the most frequent ways in which contemporary states in the Third World are permeable to foreign interests. Finally, the incumbents of the state apparatus may attempt to use their power to constitute themselves as a new class or as a distinct fraction of the dominant class. This tendency is widely visible throughout the Third World. The nature of this new class is examined at some length in the following chapters.

It should be clear that any analysis of the state in the Third World must examine the mechanisms and institutions through which social classes have access to, and influence on, the making of state policy. 'Autonomy' is perhaps best seen as referring to the degree to which policy-makers are insulated from such pressures. An examination of political forms is not sufficient; the class content of those forms must be examined. For example, it may appear (for example in Brazil) that the military and technocrats enjoy considerable autonomy in the running of the state. But if it can be shown that there exist various kinds of corporatist institutions which allow the dominant classes effectively to influence state policy, then one might conclude that the degree of autonomy enjoyed by the state apparatus from social classes is much less than appears on the surface.

A distinction must be made between state power and class power. Classes have power to the extent that their actions can have an effect on policy outcomes. This power may be expressed in many ways (strikes, threats of disorder, control over mass media, etc.). State power – the power wielded by the state apparatus – should not be confused with class power. To the extent that the state is autonomous, state power exists independently of class power.

It is certainly the case that the state in Third World countries tends to display a high level of autonomy. At the same time, state power – despite the impressive use of force which is frequently displayed – is fragile and Praetorian politics are the norm. In part this political instability is due to a series of fairly rapid shifts in the class structure and in the developmental models being pursued. Since social change occurs in a much more telescoped fashion than in the advanced capitalist countries, it is not surprising that political stability is hard to attain. At the same time, because these societies are underdeveloped and dependent, it is difficult for dominant classes to develop a great deal of legitimacy. They simply cannot deliver the goods and thereby win the acceptance of the subordinate classes. Not only do the economies have a fairly low absolute level of output but income and wealth are unequally distributed, and in addition, the economies of many underdeveloped countries are susceptible to violent fluctuations imported from the world economy.

Partly because of economic underdevelopment, and partly because of the incompleteness of the bourgeois revolution in these countries (springing from their dependent situation – of which more in the following chapter) there is very rarely a complete dominance within the power bloc of any single class or fraction. It is much more usual to find several classes or fractions sharing state power among themselves in an uneasy equilibrium. The state becomes a focus of struggle, and no class is able to develop a hegemonic position within the society as a whole. In the case of Pakistan, Hamza Alavi has argued that three social classes share state power (Alavi, 1972). A more general version of this argument has been presented for Latin America by Charles Anderson who uses the metaphor of the 'living museum' to describe Latin American states. He argues that, although new power contenders may be admitted to the political arena, as a general rule, already established actors are never pushed out entirely. As a result, it becomes increasingly difficult for the state to operate effectively (Anderson, 1967).

The achievement of hegemony requires two things: the unquestioning acceptance of the parameters of a dominant class project by subordinate classes (what might be called the legitimation of the regime) and, secondly, dominance by that class or fraction within the power bloc so that it can be sure that it controls the state apparatus.

But although the exceptional state is prevalent in the Third World, it is important to remember that there are *varieties* of exceptional state. The brittle and fragile exceptional state of pre-revolutionary Cuba, which could be toppled by a handful of middle-class insurgents, is quite different to the massive and complex apparatus of bureaucratic and technocratic domination which has been erected in Brazil in the period since 1964. Populism and techno-bureaucratic authoritarianism may both be forms of exceptional state, but they each represent distinct class projects and express distinct constellations of class forces.

The relative autonomy of the state enables it to reorganise social classes. This is most noticeable with the populist regimes, which set out to organise and incorporate subordinate social classes around a project of ISI, and seek, often successfully, to prevent the nascent proletariat from organising around its own class interests in an autonomous manner.

THE MILITARY

The military is a central part of the state apparatus. To view it as somehow 'outside' politics is frequently misleading. However, there are several kinds of military intervention in politics, and some are more 'political' than others.

The early belief, held by Edward Lieuwen among others, that a tradition of reactionary militarism was an obstacle to democracy but that, with economic development, military intervention in politics would diminish has proved over-optimistic (Lieuwen, 1962). The implied connections between a 'professional' military and an apolitical military, or between economic development *per se* and decreasing military intervention, simply do not exist.

However, the view expressed by John J. Johnson in opposition to Lieuwen, that the military could be a modernising and progressive nation-builder rather than simply an obstacle to development, also has its problems (Johnson, 1962). Johnson argued that the military was, in itself, a modern institution, a bureaucracy. It socialised recruits into the modern world, providing them with technical training, increasing literacy, and breaking down regionalism and parochialism. In addition, the military had an interest in industrialisation and were likely to support industrial development policies.

The difficulty with the views of both Lieuwen and Johnson was that they believed that 'military intervention' could be treated as an undifferentiated conceptual category. A *coup* was a *coup* was a *coup*. Clearly such an assumption is erroneous, it is a category mistake. Not all military interventions have the same causes, or the same effects. There are quite distinct types of military intervention. To attempt, as some writers have done, a statistical analysis of the causes of military intervention without a prior disaggregation of the phenomenon into types of military intervention, is not likely to produce very satisfactory or meaningful results.

Huntington has argued that one should distinguish between breakthrough *coups* – which serve to hasten history by bringing new actors into politics – and veto *coups* which resist or retard historical development. Implicit in Huntington's analysis is a theory of history which sees a sequence of development from rule by 'oligarchy' to the 'middle classes' to the 'masses'. In the 1930s, argues Huntington, the military in Latin America paved the way for the displacement of the oligarchy by the middle classes, just as in the post-war period it protected the middle-class polity against the incursions of the masses (Huntington, 1968). Unable to constitute itself as a hegemonic ruling class, the middle class is constantly threatened both by the oligarchy and by the working class, while at the same time it has to preside over a series of economic crises which increase political discontent. It survives only at the cost of a series of veto *coups* by the military. As these *coups* fail to produce a situation of economic growth and political stability, the possibility that the military will take upon itself the responsibility of government increases. This notion of a middle-class military is quite common. In addition to Huntington, versions of this theory are held by José Nún and Johnson. The question, however, is *why* does the military act in this way?

José Nún has argued that the officer corps of the Latin American military has been primarily recruited from the middle classes and this has disposed them to act as the representative of the middle classes which were too weak and heterogeneous to act effectively on their own behalf. The evidence for the assertion that the social origins of the officer corps are middle class is by no means convincing. Table 5, reproduced from A. Stepan (1971, p. 33), suggests that 78 per cent of the officer corps was of middle class origin. However, the very high degree of caste-like self-recruitment, 35 per cent of the total, should be noted. These have been included in the category 'middle class'. In addition, the criteria for differen-

TABLE 5 *Father's occupation of the 1176 cadets entering Brazilian Army Academy, 1962–6*

Traditional upper class	No.	Middle class	No.	Skilled lower class	No.	Unskilled lower class	No.
Landowner	6	Business executive	45	Electrician	9	Worker	2
Doctor	14			Craftsman	32	Peasant	2
		Military	410				
Lawyer	30			Machinist	12	Fisherman	1
		Merchant	140				
Engineer	10			Railman and	29	*Total*	5
		Civil servant	152	longshoreman		(0.4%)	
Dentist	7						
		Accountant	31	Cab and	11	Unknown	
Magistrate	3	and notary		truck driver		(Orphans)	79
							(6.7%)
Rentier	1	Bank clerk	21	Miscellaneous	8		
Total	71	Teacher	5	*Total*	101		
	(6%)				(8.6%)		
		Journalist	3				
		Druggist	7				
		Tradesman and clerk	75				
		Pensioner	5				
		Small farmer	8				
		Miscellaneous	18				
		Total	920				
			(78.2%)				

SOURCE Alfred Stepan, *The Military in Politics: Changing Patterns in Brazil* (Princeton University Press, 1971) fig. 3.2, p. 33. © 1971 by the Rand Corporation. Reprinted by permission of Princeton University Press.

tiating between 'traditional upper class' and 'middle class' are perplexing. Why an engineer is upper class and civil servants and business executives are middle class is not clear. The organisation of the data presented by Stepan needs to be treated with considerable caution. The criteria for translating occupations into class divisions appear somewhat arbitrary. Moreover, the connection between the class position of the fathers of military officers and their own action on behalf of a social class is probably more problematic than is suggested by this body of data. Nor is the use of the term 'middle class' or 'middle classes' entirely unproblematic.

I suggested in an earlier chapter that it was crucial to distinguish carefully between 'bourgeoisie' and 'middle class'. None of the writers considered here are totally unambiguous in their use of the terms.

It may be that the military supports the bourgeoisie because of their social origins in the middle class (assuming that the middle class supports the bourgeoisie), though this appears to be too direct and immediate a connection. The notion that they do so because of some structural constraint (à la Poulantzas) has previously been discarded as unhelpful. They may, on the other hand, support the bourgeoisie for ideological reasons not entirely dependent on their social origins. That is, the interests of the military as such, and the process of military socialisation, may operate to produce support for specific kinds of development projects. In this sense, the military as an institution may be relatively autonomous from class determination. The relationship between military and society is not direct.

In part, the structure and composition of the military apparatus will reflect the social structure, though never in a one-to-one relationship. However, the military always has the specific task of maintaining the existing social order. How successfully this task is carried out is, of course, problematic. Particularly in periods of transition, the internal process of socialisation which in normal times ensured adequate military role-performance may be expected to break down and the question of the class origin of the officer corps may be expected to assume greater saliency.

In some political systems, the military may adopt a moderator role *vis-à-vis* civilian politics. In this system, there are debates within the officer corps about national politics and when some kind of consensus is achieved the military will intervene in civilian politics – frequently with the consent of civilian political actors – for specific purposes. The role of the military in this kind of system is primarily to balance conflicts between actors in a predominantly Praetorian political system.

The military has, in addition, its own specific institutional interests such as the size of the defence budget, wages and the integrity of its internal hierarchy. A threat to any of these specific institutional interests may precipitate some form of military intervention.

The greater the degree to which the political system may be classified as Praetorian, the more the military is likely to intervene (a) in its own interests and (b) in a moderator role. The more the military can identify itself with a specific developmental project, the more it is likely to act in its system-maintenance role to create and defend the conditions which ensure the implementation of that project. This will occur in stable political systems in which the dominant class has developed some degree of hegemony over society. It will also occur in periods of transition, when an ascendent social class is challenging the incumbent dominant class. In such transitional conjunctures, the military, if it adopts the new developmental project, may either relinquish power to a civilian leadership (even though individual military officers may form part of the government) or may itself as an institution take over the running of the government. Whether it returns or retains power, and whether it expands or restricts political participation, will depend on the nature of the development project and the correlation of class forces.

Crisis *coups* – where the military intervenes in its system-maintenance role either to defend the dominant class against a threat of revolution or to replace one class project with another – are much less frequent than moderator *coups* (which are a regular occurrence in Praetorian political systems). They are however much more important. For a crisis *coup* to take place, both the opportunity for the military to act, and its own capacity to act must be simultaneously present. The opportunity is a function of crisis in the political system; the military's ability to intervene will depend on its own internal cohesion around a specific programme. The military is very rarely a monolithic bloc. The process of building up support for a *coup* is sometimes quite difficult. It is complicated by the (normal) need to observe military hierarchy. At which point in the chain of command a *coup* is mounted is a central issue. Moreover, the military is usually split along vertical lines between the different branches of the armed forces and sometimes between different territorial jurisdictions. The Brazilian Army, for example, is divided into four distinct armies, located in different parts of the country. In 1961, when there was a possibility of a *coup* being mounted to depose president-elect Goulart, the Third Army in Rio Grande do Sul, comprising about one-third of the army's total strength, refused to go along with the preparations for a *coup*, and the rest of the army backed down.

The process of building a coalition within the military for a *coup* does not depend simply on numbers and on chains of command. Purely military considerations are also important. Control of the armoured division, or of key garrisons, may be sufficient to convince the rest of the army that if push came to shove, they would be on the losing side. In such a situation it would be most unusual for those with the inferior firepower not to acquiesce and join with the stronger side. Armies very rarely divide and fight each other in civil-war type scenarios.

9

Revolution

Marx had put forward a powerful argument to the effect that the internal contradictions of capitalism would create the conditions for the seizure of state power by the industrial working class and the transformation of society in a socialist direction. The proletariat in the places where capitalism was most advanced (Europe and the United States) would be the bearer of the socialist revolution. In the century since Marx put forward this argument this proletarian revolution has *not* occurred in the advanced capitalist nations, while the industrially less developed nations, beginning with Russia in 1917, have witnessed revolution upon revolution and the construction of socialist states. Moreover, with the possible exception of the Russian Revolution, the industrial proletariat has played a relatively minor role in these revolutions.

Growing out of this series of developments unanticipated in the writings of the classical Marxists (that is, pre-Lenin) has been a continuous process of modification of the original corpus of Marxist theory. The point at which these later modifications transform Marxism into a doctrine totally dissimilar from the one held by Marx himself is, particularly from the point of view of political action, an important issue for debate. Unfortunately, I do not have the space to deal with it more than in passing here.

The initial attempts to accommodate the fact of the Russian Revolution to the theoretical heritage of Marxism focused on the European context of the revolution. Both Lenin and Trotsky emphasised that the seizure of state power in Russia by a party of the working class was merely the opening act of the European revolution. Unless the industrial proletariat in Western Europe also made a revolution, the Soviet Union would be isolated and, owing to its backwardness, would not be able to move forward to socialism. A counter-revolution would occur.

Why had the socialist revolution first broken out in backward Russia? Essentially, because it was the weak link in the chain of European capitalism. Trotsky, who developed a more complex analysis than Lenin, argued that despite the rapid growth of large-scale industry, and the emergence of a modern proletariat, the Russian bourgeoisie had failed to seize the state apparatus from the Tsarist autocracy. It could only do so by enlisting the aid of the working class, but it feared the working class and consequently vacillated between its desire to control the state and its terror of unleashing a revolution. In this situation, argued Trotsky, the task of the working class was to push the bourgeoisie, however unwillingly, into a revolution and then carry that revolution through the bourgeois stage into the stage of a socialist revolution by presenting its own demands and making an alliance with the numerically powerful peasantry (Trotsky, 1931).

This theory of permanent revolution had its origins in some of Marx's writings on the Paris Commune. It differed fundamentally from the view held by the Mensheviks and by many orthodox Marxists that only after the successful completion of the bourgeois revolution could the proletariat begin to press forward its own demands. Until that time, all that Marxists could do was to support the bourgeoisie in its struggle with the Tsarist autocracy. The revolution, according to this conception, was to be made in stages.

Trotsky's theory of the running together of the two stages argued, however, that while the backwardness of Russia made such a revolution possible, that very backwardness also constituted a grave danger in the event that a revolution in the West was not forthcoming. The absence of the revolution in the West would inevitably mean the destruction of the Russian Revolution.

Trotsky was wrong. The revolution in the West failed to materialise and yet there was no restoration of capitalism in the Soviet Union. Instead, there was a fantastic drive towards industrial growth during the Stalinist period and the development of a new dominant class. (The nature of this class – and, indeed, whether it is actually a *class* – is the subject of considerable debate. For my purposes, an exact definition of the nature of the Soviet dominant class is unnecessary. I return to the subject in the following chapter, though even there I do not give the subject the space it deserves.)

The immensity of the Soviet achievement became visible in the 1940s, at the same time that (a) Eastern Europe came under

Soviet domination and (b) the Chinese Revolution neared the final stages of its development. In the meanwhile, under the aegis of Joseph Stalin, Marxism had been subjected to a number of transmutations, foremost of which was the doctrine of 'socialism in one country'. The effect of the assertion (a) that socialism could be built in a single, backward country and (b) that the Soviet Union was, in some real sense, a socialist society was to divert Marxism from a concern for the self-emancipation of the proletariat to a recipe for the emancipation of the productive forces. Under Stalin, socialism came to mean economic planning and state ownership (Harris, 1968).

The importance of this transformation of Marxist theory is that it was a version of Stalinism, together with the unique contributions made by the Chinese and Cuban revolutions and the liberation struggles in Africa and Asia, which gained predominance in the countries of the Third World. The implication of this will be considered shortly.

The principal contribution of the Russian Revolution in its Stalinist form had been to destroy the notion of the proletariat as the new, temporarily dominant class. The contribution of the Chinese Revolution, as expressed in Maoism, was to take this process one step further and deny the working class any role in the organisation of the revolution itself.

This was logical enough after the debacle of the 1927 uprising in Shanghai during which the Chinese Communist Party's base in the industrial working class was smashed utterly. Thereafter, the Party operated almost exclusively in the countryside until the final victory of the revolution in 1949. But although the working class had played no role in the revolution, the Chinese leadership continued to describe their revolution as 'proletarian'. The word changed its meaning; it no longer referred in any way to a specific social class; rather it identified a particular constellation of ideological themes.

The peasantry had played an important role in the Chinese Revolution and increasingly came to be seen by revolutionaries as the revolutionary class *par excellence*. Marx's derogatory remarks about the reactionary nature of the French smallholding peasantry of the nineteenth century, and the Russian conflicts with the Kulaks (cf. Lewin, 1968) dropped out of sight and, in the post-war world, many theorists turned to the peasantry as the principal revolutionary force.

This embrace of the peasantry was facilitated by a none-too-complex analysis of the internal differentiation of the peasantry. The categories of 'poor', 'middle' and 'rich' peasant practically exhausted Maoism's theoretical vocabulary. As we saw in Chapter 7, such a simplistic notion of the rural social structure was not likely to offer much in the way of an accurate understanding of social reality, much less a guide to successful revolutionary action. Nevertheless, Marxism – now in its Maoist variant – had nearly completed its long march from a theory of the self-emancipation of the industrial working class to a voluntaristic recipe for rural insurrection followed by state planning and capital accumulation.

But while the theory of peasant revolution marked a stage in this process of theoretical transformation, it did not represent the ultimate step in the direction of voluntarism. The final abandonment of revolutionary theory conceived of as an analysis of the dynamics of the social structure which could serve as a guide for revolutionary action, came in the aftermath of the Cuban Revolution and the Algerian independence movement. It was the task of theorists like Franz Fanon and Regis Debray to divorce revolutionary practice totally from revolutionary theory.

Simultaneously, the development of the theory of dependency was generating exactly the same result. It did so by means of a combination of a concern for economic growth and a theory of revolution not dissimilar to the prognoses of 'marginality theory'. The theory of revolution implicit in certain radical dependency theorists, such as A. G. Frank, asserted that only those sectors of society which were excluded from full participation, those strata at the very bottom of the social pyramid, had any revolutionary potential. The result was a justification of revolution as a necessary condition for economic development.

The origins of the dependency paradigm in the ECLA critique of Latin America's inability to generate an internally-oriented process of economic growth, together with the impact of the Cuban Revolution, meant that the notion of a 'socialist revolution' emphasised primarily the potential liberation of the forces of production. In common with a familiar post-Stalin transformation of Marxism in the Third World, socialism, for these radical theorists of underdevelopment, came increasingly to be viewed as a recipe for economic growth rather than as the self-emancipation of the working class. As economic growth and capital accumulation took the centre of the stage, the notion of the 'proletariat' became increasingly divorced from any association with the industrial working class.

The rationale for a socialist revolution stemmed from the imperatives of capital accumulation, rather than from the felt needs of the working class to transcend its situation of exploitation and alienation. Agreeing with ECLA economists on the need for structural transformations in order to generate economic growth, the dependency theorists showed (correctly) that the interests of the ruling class in the countries of the Third World lay in a preservation of the *status quo* and in opposition to reforms. Hence, if there were to be economic development, the existing ruling classes would have to be overthrown and replaced by an elite committed to rapid economic growth. In dependency theory, socialist revolution takes the place of technocratic incrementalism. Again, the Stalinist equation of socialism with economic planning and state ownership of the means of production is reproduced.

These arguments may well prove persuasively the need for a revolution but it is more than a mere semantic quibble when we ask why this revolution is described as 'socialist'. True, Western Marxists also argued that the social relations of production would act as fetters on the further development of the productive forces. But there was rather more to it than economic growth *per se*. The working class was to emancipate itself (and at the same time create the conditions for the emancipation of all other classes) from exploitation and alienation, not merely move from poverty to affluence. This is not to suggest that economic growth is not an urgent and pressing problem for the underdeveloped countries. Rather, what is at issue is whether this transition can accurately be described as socialism. Paul Baran has suggested that 'socialism in backward and underdeveloped countries has a powerful tendency to become a backward and underdeveloped socialism' (Baran, 1957, p. viii).

The socialism which exists in many countries of the Third World is indeed a lumpensocialism. What exists is a form of class rule in which the historical task of capital accumulation (abdicated by the bourgeoisie) is performed by a bureaucratic elite drawn from diverse petty bourgeois sectors. This elite retains state power through the most varied forms of corruption, nepotism and repression while it attempts to consolidate itself into a new capitalist class. Isaac

Deutscher's comment on Stalin's forced industrialisation can also be applied to this notion of a socialist revolution for development:

> Marx sums up his picture of the English industrial revolution by saying that 'capital comes into the world dripping from head to foot, from every pore, with blood and dirt.' Thus also comes into the world – socialism in one country. (Deutscher, 1966, p. 340)

Thus it is that a lumpentheory of lumpendevelopment produces in its turn a lumpensolution of lumpensocialism. The confusions stem from the analysis of social classes and from the assimilation of the social relations internal to the social formations of dependent societies to the model of colonial relations.

There is not a great deal to be said about the theories of Fanon and Debray. They each present remarkably perceptive analyses of the situation of underdevelopment and each end up by posing the question of revolution in purely moral and voluntaristic terms. For Debray, the objective conditions for revolution already exist in the Third World; all that is needed is catalyst – a little motor to start the big motor. Such a catalyst can be found in the guerrilla *foco*, whose very existence will be the single spark that sets the prairie aflame (Debray, 1967).

Drawing on the example of Cuba, Debray saw Latin American states as fundamentally weak and exposed, continuing to exist only because they were propped up by imperialism. This may well have been true of pre-1959 Cuba and of some other countries, but as a universal description it was wide of the mark. There may well have been a generalised crisis of hegemony throughout the underdeveloped world, but the extent of the crisis varied greatly from country to country. By failing to examine the class structure and political institutions at greater length, Debray fell into the voluntarist error of supposing that all that was needed was to pick up a gun and take to the hills. The dismal experience of the guerrillas in latin America in the 1960s attests to the fatuity of such a proposition.

Other theorists turned their gaze on different candidates for the role of revolutionary vanguard. Some, like Fanon, looked to the lumpenproletariat of the rapidly-growing shanty towns; others believed they saw in sections of the military a progressive force

(the Peruvian experience was one of the sources of this vision);
while some, such as A. Cabral, saw in the petty bourgeoisie the
only force which could lead a revolution.

But, as Cabral realised, leadership of the revolution by the petty
bourgeoisie might result in the creation of a new form of class
dictatorship. To avoid this, it would be necessary for the petty
bourgeois leadership of the revolution to renounce voluntarily such
a possibility. It would have to commit suicide as a class (Cabral,
1969). In view of the experience of the last few decades, one
does not need to be much of a sceptic to question the likelihood
of such a self-sacrifice.

All these theorists of revolution saw themselves as working within
a Marxist framework. Yet despite all the differences between them,
they all held in common a belief that the industrial working class
was not the vanguard of the revolution. Some, indeed, went on
to claim that the working class in underdeveloped countries was
in essence a labour aristocracy, a privileged elite whose politics
were inevitably conservative.

The notion of an aristocracy of labour has enjoyed considerable
support among many theorists who trace the origin of the concept
back to remarks made by Engels and later by Lenin about the
British working class. Over time, the concept has become quite
diffuse. Some writers refer to a particular *stratum* of the working
class, while others apparently accept that the working class as
a whole may reasonably be described as a labour aristocracy.
In Lenin's version, the term was used to refer to a stratum of
the working class that had been bought off by the proceeds from
empire and had adopted a conservative political stance. There
are a number of difficulties with this theory. In the first place,
it is by no means easy to identify a stratum of the working class
which is in receipt of imperial tribute as opposed to a stratum
which is not. The connection between imperialism and high working-class income is not at all clear. Secondly, the evidence for
a correlation between income and conservatism within the working
class is not entirely unambiguous either. Any theory of working-class
political behaviour must be more complex and must take account
of changing occupational structures, occupational mobility and of
institutional processes (such as the formation of trade unions and
political parties).

It may well be (or not, as the case may be) that there is

no longer (and perhaps never was) any revolutionary potential in the industrial working class in the advanced capitalist countries. But simply to transfer such a conclusion to the industrial proletariat of the countries of the Third World is to ignore the considerable structural differences which exist and which form part of any theory of working-class politics. Even if no comparison is intended, even if it is argued on the basis of evidence from the Third World alone that the working class is a conservative political force, the evidence as such cannot admit such a straightforward conclusion. The role of the working class in revolutionary movements in Cuba, Chile, Argentina and Bolivia simply cannot be ignored.

Clearly the notion of a labour aristocracy is but a feeble substitute for a serious analysis of the structural factors disposing the working class towards political radicalism. It is not, however, the intention here to assert that the industrial proletariat always and everywhere has a revolutionary vocation. On the contrary, as this book has repeatedly argued, the politics of any social class, group or stratum are a function not only of the structural characteristics of the class itself, but also of the structure of the field of action into which that class is inserted.

Considerations such as these suggest some of the problems involved in using the terms 'proletarian revolution' or 'socialist revolution' without precision. The very concept of 'revolution' is itself highly problematic. The term might refer to the seizure of state power or, alternatively, it might refer to the process of structural transformation from one type of society to another. The relationship between the moment of insurrectionary seizure of state power and the process of structural transformation is by no means simple. It is *not* the case, as some crude versions of Marxism have it, that the passage from one mode of production to another is always marked by a dramatic rupture in the state form. The transformation of the class character of the state apparatus has its own specific dynamics.

Even when the sense of the term 'revolution' is clear, the addition of an adjectival prefix such as 'socialist' or 'proletarian' could mean one of several things. These words might refer to the actors, to the leadership, to the ideology or to the outcome of the revolution. For example, when we talk of the 'bourgeois' revolution we may mean a revolution that hastens the development of capitalism or a revolution led by the bourgeoisie, or to some combination of these phenomena.

In many current versions of Marxism, 'proletarian revolution' has lost its original meaning of a revolution carried out by the proletariat to establish socialism, and has come to mean simply a process which results in the creation of a state committed to some form of economic planning, state ownership and economic growth. When these are features of nearly all forms of contemporary economic systems it is hardly surprising that 'socialism' is so widespread. The class nature of these regimes needs, however, to be examined with more care, and it is to this task that we turn in the following chapter.

One of the results in this shift in the meaning of the term is the phenomenon of the 'accidental' discovery that a regime is 'socialist'. Cuba provides a good example. In the period before their victory, it would be difficult to find evidence of any socialistic programme in the statements of the Cuban revolutionaries. The vast majority of Cuban revolutionaries – and this definitely includes the group around Fidel Castro – sought three interrelated goals: the overthrow of the Batista dictatorship and the establishment of some form of parliamentary democracy; diminished dependence on the United States; and diminished dependence on sugar and a serious programme of economic development. This was a programme essentially the same as that put forward by José Martí at the turn of the century (Ruiz, 1968).

It was only in 1961, nearly three years after the Rebel Army drove into Havana, that Fidel Castro declared in public that the revolution was socialist. This development of 'socialism without socialists' requires some explanation. One interpretation of Cuban history suggests that Castro 'betrayed' what was, in essence, a middle-class revolution, arguing that Castro had held socialist views all along (Draper, 1965). This conspiratorial theory appears to have little basis in reality. More realistic is the proposition that the hostile moves by the US Government forced Castro's hand and left him no alternative to massive expropriation of farms and industries. Against this view, James O'Connor argues plausibly that such a result could only have occurred if the revolutionary leadership had been (as they were) genuinely committed to economic development (O'Connor, 1970b). In that case, the logic of underdevelopment left them no option but state ownership and economic planning. In O'Connor's view, there was a necessary evolution to socialism. Because socialism was – as the dependency theorists have argued – a necessary condition for economic development, a leadership committed to economic development necessarily became socialist. To assume that the actions of the United States would have had any other result than to obstruct that development would be to fly in the face of history.

But is revolution a necessary condition for development, as neo-Marxists such as Paul Baran and the dependency theorists argue? Clearly certain forms of economic development *are* possible without revolution. Even if Brazil's economic growth in the period after 1964 is labelled 'associated dependent development' (Cardoso, 1973) it is still development. Although the costs may be fantastically high, it is difficult to accept *in toto* the arguments put forward by theorists such as Baran and Frank that there is no growth at all in (at least some) underdeveloped countries. Even dependent countries can develop, though their dependency may increase and the cost may be high.

Nevertheless, it does seem reasonable to accept that a revolution may – by endowing an elite committed to economic growth with state power and popular legitimacy – vastly enhance the probability that development will occur. The obstacles put in the way of development by private vested interests, both domestic and foreign, may be greatly reduced and the altered correlation of class forces may give the revolutionary leadership sufficient freedom of action to create new institutions more propitious to a development effort. However, other obstacles will remain, and there is no guarantee of success. Again, Cuba provides a useful example.

In addition to the difficulties noted in Chapter 3 facing a country which wishes to move away from reliance on a single agricultural export (and Argentina is another good example), Cuba also faced a number of problems directly deriving from the revolutionary experience. There was a great shortage of technical expertise, which is a feature of all underdeveloped societies, but which was compounded by the mass exodus of many professionals to the United States. Moreover, there was bound to be an initial period of costly experimentation with new forms of organisation. Decision-making procedures were only slowly regularised. In this process, Fidel's personal intervention – however much it may have built up legitimacy for the new regime – seems, on balance, to have been a considerable hindrance (Dumont, 1973). Even today, some twenty years after the revolution in Cuba, the process of institutionalisation is still far from complete.

10

Varieties of Bourgeois Revolution

The argument presented throughout this book has been that there is a strong trend, in the societies of the Third World, towards the establishment of state forms which are exceptional. The weakness of any domestic bourgeoisie in these countries has enabled the elites which have come to occupy state power to transform themselves into new dominant classes. This chapter will examine this phenomenon at some length and will attempt to specify the nature of these new classes. To do so I will return to the debate about a 'progressive national bourgeoisie'.

As was noted in Chapter 6, the view held by the Communist Parties in the inter-war period (and in some parts of the Third World this view has survived into the contemporary epoch) was in many ways a reformulation of the Menshevik position. In order for economic development to occur, the national bourgeoisie had to take power from the landed oligarchy and the comprador bourgeoisie (in an anti-developmental alliance with imperialism). The task of the proletariat and other subordinate classes was to support this progressive national bourgeoisie. Thus, development was seen as bourgeois development. The tasks of the bourgeois revolution – the creation of a viable nation-state and a process of autonomous capital accumulation – still remained to be carried out.

However, with a few possible exceptions, no bourgeoisie stepped forward to take power and carry out these tasks. But the incomplete and dependent nature of the development of capitalism in the Third World was a constant source of social tension. The introduction of capitalism had created tensions, but the very incompleteness of the capitalist transformation compounded them.

In terms of the organisation of a nation-state, the tasks of the bourgeois revolution were incomplete because the states of those societies remained highly *permeable*. Their state structures were open to penetration by imperialist powers, and could not be relied on to serve national purposes. Secondly, the domination of the state over civil society was often incomplete; much remained outside the aegis of the state. In this sense, the states of the Third World were often quite weak in terms of their power to organise civil society. Thirdly, and perhaps most importantly, these states exhibited a lack of hegemony. The perpetual crisis of hegemony facing the states of the Third World resulted in frequent, but partial, attempts at revolution. These attempts at revolution, because of the weakness of the social forces involved, usually meant some form of accommodation and compromise with the classes supporting the *ancien régime*. In terms of policy, the result was a constant paralysis and stalemate. The reforms necessary for the successful completion of a development programme were rarely enacted.

The tasks of the bourgeois revolution were also unfulfilled in the economic sphere. This was, of course, glaringly obvious in the unsatisfactory rates of capital accumulation, the extreme vulnerability to external influences, and the inability to establish any kind of autocentric development. As both cause and consequence of the crippling effects of dependency, the bourgeoisie was stunted in its growth as a social class. It simply could not (with some exceptions) act as an autonomous class with its own development project.

Thus, while the tasks of the bourgeois revolution remained unfulfilled, the bourgeoisie itself abdicated any pretensions to a revolutionary role. Barrington Moore's first route to modernisation – bourgeois revolution from below – was foreclosed. Some other class, or class alliance, had to take on its shoulders the task of modernisation.

One possible option was what Moore calls 'revolution from above' and Gramsci termed 'passive revolution'. Both were referring to fascist-led attempts at modernisation. The term, however, may be used more generally to refer to any attempt by an elite other than the bourgeoisie to use its control of the state to oversee an attempt at rapid economic development in which, by and large, bourgeois property is not totally expropriated. The terms would then include certain kinds of military regimes such as the Nasserite regime in Egypt and the Peruvian military government after 1968.

The relationship between these political elites and the bourgeoisie is often complex and fraught with tension. These regimes often expropriate substantial sectors of the economy and often attempt to control the bourgeoisie through a variety of corporatist institutions. Nevertheless, they are rarely opposed to private enterprise as such, and often develop close relations with at least some sectors of the bourgeoisie.

However, in the extreme case, these regimes of revolution from above can totally displace the bourgeoisie (particularly where the bourgeoisie is very new or very weak) and may then create a new state bourgeoisie. In this case, political groups within the state will parcel out economic enterprises in a patrimonial manner. Corruption, clientelism and a dispersal of state power into private 'feuds' is a likely result. This kind of political system is quite different from those set up by a 'revolution from below' led by the Communist Party. In these cases, the centralisation of economy and polity make the appearance of patrimonialism unlikely.

Nevertheless, despite the differences, all these regimes have one thing in common: they all arise out of the attempt by some social class or political elite to carry through the tasks of the bourgeois revolution. Here Trotsky's notion of permanent revolution may be useful. But instead of the proletariat pushing the bourgeoisie on to revolution and then carrying the revolution one stage further, some other social force takes over the role of the proletariat. In this arrested or deflected permanent revolution, the bureaucracy or the petty bourgeoisie leads the revolution. Once in power, a Bonapartist congealing of mass mobilisation occurs, as the new holders of state power seek to consolidate their control over society. The ability of the petty bourgeoisie or a bureaucratic apparatus to substitute itself for the bourgeoisie or for the working class is a function of the weakness and lack of cohesion of social forces in the society. Once in power, the way in which the new elite begins to transform itself into a new class can vary. Several forms of class alliance are possible (Shivji, 1976). In this chapter, we will examine this process in terms of the debate over the timing of the bourgeois revolution in Latin America.

According to the majority of Marxist theorists, since the transition from one mode of production to another requires a correlative change in the organisation of political life and the displacement of one ruling class by another, then this transition is bound to be marked by a sharp discontinuity in the form of political domination, by a revolution. If Latin America has witnessed a shift from feudalism to capitalism, then we must direct our efforts toward the analysis of the bourgeois revolution.

> If we must look for bourgeois democratic revolution and industrialization efforts in Latin America at all, we should do so during the period roughly between 1825 and 1860. During this period almost all of Latin America experienced a series of civil wars. (Frank, 1972, p. 31)

Frank has suggested that these civil wars were fought out principally over the issue of Latin America's definitive integration into the imperialist world market. This interpretation has much in common with the position put forward by one of Frank's critics, Vania Bambirra. She dates the dominance of the capitalist mode of production in Latin America from the time of its incorporation into the world market after 1850 (Bambirra, 1973, p. 36). However, in Frank's interpretation, these struggles do not constitute an authentic bourgeois revolution (how could they if Latin American societies had always been capitalist?) but were rather a lumpenbourgeois counter-revolution (Frank, 1972, p. 15). The success of this lumpenbourgeoisie was a key factor in the creation and perpetuation of underdevelopment in Latin America.

But if there was no authentic bourgeois revolution, then we are faced with the dilemma of a capitalism without a bourgeois revolution. There are three ways out. In the first place, following Trotsky's theory of the permanent revolution, we might conclude that while the tasks of the bourgeois revolution remain to be carried out, the bourgeoisie itself will not fulfil this task, and some other class must substitute for the bourgeoisie and then proceed to carry through its own programme (Trotsky, 1931). Unlike Trotsky, we believe that there are other classes besides the proletariat which can carry through the tasks of the bourgeois revolution. Foremost among these is the radical petty bourgeoisie. When this happens, when the tasks of the bourgeoisie are assumed by a class other than the proletariat, the path of the permanent revolution is deflected (Cliff, 1963), and the result is not socialism but rather what has been called in this book, 'lumpensocialism'.

The alternative (though not necessarily an exclusive one) would be to argue that the mode of production in Latin America is neither feudal nor capitalist, but rather a new mode of production. The advantage of this procedure is that it explains the absence of the bourgeois revolution. For the sake of convenience we could call this new mode of production the 'dependent mode of production'. However, a label is not an explanation.

Just as the meaning of the concept of bourgeois revolution becomes problematic when applied to peripheral and dependent societies, so also does its dating. Of course, it is extremely difficult, except with a highly restricted definition, to locate precisely the transition from feudalism to capitalism in Western Europe. Scholars have difficulty pinning the transition period down to anything less than two or three centuries, and though they may argue that there existed certain pivotal conjunctures, only a few would argue that an abrupt and total transition actually occurred. (The most usual line of argument here concerns the seizure of state power by the bourgeoisie and the transformation of the nature of the state into a bourgeois state apparatus. However, even this apparently abrupt change appears not to have occurred in any straightforward fashion, being marked rather by anticipatory developments (the feudal absolutist state) and by a whole series of compromises between the forces of the old order and the representatives of the new.)

If the problem of dating looms so large for the societies of the original transition, the very same problem must necessarily be magnified for the dependent and peripheral societies which, by virtue of their dependency, have been unable to repeat this historically unique transition. For these societies, the bourgeois revolution presents itself not as a single phenomenon, a unique historical experience of transition, but rather in a disaggregated form as a constellation of discrete tasks to be carried out separately, often at quite different times and in quite different epochs. However, this very separateness implies an incompleteness, in two different ways. The revolution is always incomplete to the extent that only some of its tasks are fulfilled at any given time. What in the West happened in an abbreviated space of historical time is now spread thinly across the events of centuries. The revolution is incomplete in the sense that it is not yet finished; the accomplishments are only partial. At the same time, this form of incompleteness gives rise to the second: to an inability fully to carry through even the partial tasks attempted. Not only is it the case that only some of the historic tasks of the bourgeois revolution are ever attempted at any given time, but even those that are attempted are rarely successfully carried through to completion. Democracy and the formation of the nation remain always provisory achievements, constantly subject to interruption and historical retrogression. Economic emancipation is always frustrated and turned back into ever newer forms of dependency and exploitation. In the historical development of the Third World, each form of incompleteness feeds on and intensifies the other.

Where, then, do we begin in an attempt to locate the phases of the bourgeois revolution in Latin America? In the view of Frank and Wallerstein the key fact is the incorporation of the periphery into the expanding capitalist world economic system of the sixteenth and seventeenth centuries. In terms of their definitions, once integrated into the networks of commercial trade, these societies must be characterised as capitalist. Yet within that framework, their position and role in the international system undergo successive transformations. The struggle for independence from Spain and Portugal, the civil wars of the early post-independence period, the transformation of the internal productive structures into specialised primary-commodity export sectors in the late nineteenth century, the 'turn inwards' and the attempts at import-substitution industrialisation in the 1930s and 1940s, the take-off into rapid growth of a few of the larger economies in the post-war period (Brazil and Mexico), are all possible candidates for the label 'bourgeois revolution'.

The third alternative is to stress the continuing and incomplete nature of the transformation. The world capitalist system is continually going through a series of transformations, which have a profound impact in the countries of the Third World. The relations between centre and periphery continually undergo structural shifts. The change from an export-orientation to ISI and then to the dominance of the multinationals are examples of the principal transformations which have taken place in Latin America. Each structural shift in the economy brought with it a changing realignment of class forces and political turmoil. In this sense, the bourgeois revolution has been a continuous process in Latin America. One cannot therefore give it a precise date, one can only point to the various phases of the process.

Once it is accepted that 'the bourgeois revolution' in the countries of the Third World is a process rather than a single event, a reanalysis of the class nature of contemporary popular revolutions and revolutionary movements becomes indispensable.

Speaking in the most general terms, it is possible to discern a watershed in the development of revolutionary prospects in Latin America in the decade of the 1950s. During the period between the world economic depression of the 1930s and the recovery of the capitalist world economy under US dominance in the post Second World War period, attempts at revolution and at autonomous development in Latin America were dominated, implicitly or explicitly, by the notion of a progressive and autonomous national bourgeois development. This period saw several important attempts at economic development which were accompanied by various forms of populist mobilisation under the political leadership of the industrial bourgeoisie. Examples are such phenomena as the Estado Nôvo in Brazil, Peronism in Argentina, the Popular Front Government in Chile, the rise of APRA in Peru, etc. Of course, all these movements were highly complex, and the alliances of classes and the forms in which bourgeois dominance of the coalitions was expressed varied greatly from country to country. Nevertheless, speaking in these global terms, it seems reasonable to make the general assertion that during this period the progressive and revolutionary movements, and revolutionary thought, were predominantly under the influence of the new industrial bourgeoisie which was benefiting from the process of import-substitution industrialisation.

The situation changed dramatically with the post-war imperialist offensive. The feasibility of bourgeois reformist attempts at development was seriously reduced, and specifically socialist parties and programmes began to play an increasingly important role *vis-à-vis* nationalist and petty bourgeois elements. The situation did not, of course, change overnight, and in a great many ways, radical petty bourgeois ideologies continued to exert a strong influence within the revolutionary movements.

BOLIVIA

The Bolivian Revolution of 1952 may be considered as an almost pure attempt at a bourgeois revolution. Pre-revolutionary Bolivia was dominated by three big tin-mining enterprises – the Patiño, Aramayo and Hochschild groups – collectively known as the Rosca. With very few linkages to the rest of the economy, tin was the country's principal export and must be characterised as an economic enclave. This group of tin magnates did not rule directly. Providing that the interests of tin were not challenged, a stratum of petty bourgeois bureaucrats was left to run the affairs of the state, while in the countryside the *hacendado* class maintained the peasantry in a servile and apolitical status.

The frustrations and bitterness growing out of the Chaco war of 1932–5 and the slow economic growth after 1925 led to the increasing articulation of middle class discontent and increased intra-elite conflict over the distribution of wealth and power. The ensuing political instability led to attempted solutions in the direction of military-sponsored corporatism in the 1930s; attempts which, in the final analysis, failed and merely served to exacerbate the growing political instability. The continuing growth of the labour movement and the increasing militancy of the tin miners contributed to the steady expansion of political conflict.

By 1949 the recently-formed middle-class party, the MNR (Movimiento Nacionalista Revolucionario) had formed an alliance with the Trotskyist POR (Partido Obrero Revolucionario) and had embarked on attempts at seizure of state power by a combination of insurrection and *coup d'état*. In 1952, thanks to the successful action of the workers, and after a short period of fighting with the army, the MNR eventually came to power. The army was largely disbanded, arms were distributed to workers and peasants, the peasants began to take over the land, the COB (Central Obrera Boliviana) was formed, and a brief period of MNR–POR dual power began.

The relative ease with which the existing power incumbents were dislodged and the military was effectively destroyed as part of the state apparatus is to be explained by the absence of any organic links between the Rosca and the state apparatus. The tin magnates may have benefited greatly from the existing set-up, and in a sense it would be true to say that the state acted on their behalf to protect their interests, but they were never a ruling class. The evidence suggests that the Rosca were not directly involved in the running of the state apparatus, and there were few, if any, organic ties between the tin magnates and the bureaucrats and politicians who actually ran the state apparatus. For this reason, the state was relatively fragile and vulnerable. Moreover, the institutions of civil society were weak and incapable of coming to the defence of the threatened social order. There was in Bolivia in 1952 an almost complete *absence* of hegemony.

Once in power the MNR faced the dual task of consolidating its political position and implementing a coherent development strategy. The two tasks were, naturally, closely tied together. In the first heady days of the revolution, something approximating a situation of dual power existed. The government was dominated by the MNR, with the Trotskyist-controlled COB having an important minority voice. With the nationalisation of the tin mines and the dispossession of the latifundistas as a result of the agrarian reform, the MNR regime faced few important internal enemies. The power of the army had been greatly reduced, and there now existed armed militias of workers and peasants. Given this situation, the regime could have moved sharply to the left, the POR could have increased its power, and the revolution might have passed on to a socialist stage, following the schema laid out by Trotsky in his theory of the permanent revolution. This did not happen, and as a result of the economic development programme chosen, the regime gradually shifted to the right, confronting the working class at a number of key points, and consolidating a bourgeois state apparatus.

Two economic problems faced the MNR regime in its early days: declining revenue from its major export, tin; and rapid inflation. The response of the centre–left government of Paz Estenssoro was to placate the potential middle-class opposition represented by the FSB (Falange Socialista Boliviana), introduce a stabilisation plan sponsored by the IMF, and accept the costs of increasing conflict with the miners and organised working class.

Nevertheless, the political stalemate was not broken, and the economy continued to stagnate. The centre–right administration of Hernan Siles (1956–60) set about breaking out of the deadlock. The principal problem was the COB, virtually a state within a state. Its autonomy had to be destroyed. The army was gradually rebuilt and the MNR consolidated its control over the peasant militias, grouping them together under regional *caudillos*. This process took some time, and it was only with the return of Paz to the presidency in 1960 that the deadlock was finally broken.

In 1961 the Triangular Plan was signed between Bolivia and the United States, the IMF and West Germany. This plan provided foreign capital and resources for the modernisation of the tin mines in return for a commitment on the part of the regime to restore labour discipline in the mines. The MNR carried out its part of the bargain. In 1963 units of the army aided by peasant militias surrounded the chief mining centres and forced the miners to capitulate.

The irony of this story is that Paz strengthened the army to break the power of the workers; once this task had been accomplished the army then turned against the MNR, overthrowing it in 1964, and attempted to implement its own development strategy.

Once the choice of a development strategy had been made, the political confrontation with the working class was unavoidable. Why then did the MNR choose a development path based on increased exports of tin and on continued co-operation with the United States? After all, the Soviet Union offered in 1960 to provide Bolivia with the funds to build its own smelter, thereby increasing its independence *vis-à-vis* the United States. The answer lies in the fact that if the Bolivian regimes had moved significantly to the left, the MNR might have had to yield power to its working-class rival, the POR. Faced with an organised working class on its left, the bourgeois MNR could not radicalise its position and still be sure of retaining state power. The MNR opted for state-guided development within the international capitalist system, but failed in the event to achieve any reasonable degree of sound economic growth. Faced with the dilemma of economic growth (requiring accumulation) versus popular support (requiring increases in popular consumption), and given the existence of potential challengers for state power, the choice in favour of growth and accumulation led inexorably to repression and political confrontation, led eventually to the demise of the MNR regime at the hands of its own creation, the Bolivian army.

CUBA

If the Bolivian Revolution was a pathetic failure, clearly the Cuban Revolution which came seven years later has been a success. Perhaps a qualified success, but success all the same. Yet when the Rebel Army marched into Havana in January 1959, there was no reason to assume that the course of events would greatly differ from what happened in Bolivia. The programmatic statement of the 26 July movement – Fidel Castro's speech at his trial, *History Will Absolve Me* (Castro, 1962) – does not go beyond the boundaries of progressive bourgeois thought. It is firmly situated within a tradition of radical nationalist thought whose organisational expression was the bourgeois Ortodoxo party and has its roots in Jose Marti's writings during Cuba's struggle for independence. This was characteristic of Cuban radical thought: it was formulated principally in terms of a struggle for national independence. This meant, in the Cuba of the 1950s, the overthrow of the Batista dictatorship, establishment of bourgeois democracy, and a move away from Cuba's dependence on sugar and on the United States.

Castro's methods of struggle – guerrilla warfare – may have been radical, but this does not mean that they were socialist. Recently, there have been attempts (Bambirra, 1973; Bray and Harding, 1974) to show that the Rebel Army was composed largely of workers and peasants, and that it had important links with the urban working class. This may or may not be the case. The evidence is not convincing. More importantly, the social composition of the Rebel Army is only one factor (and quite a minor one at that) in determining the class character of the Cuban Revolution.

The leadership of the Rebel Army was not drawn from the peasantry or from the working class, and more importantly, the class content of its political programme (while popular in character) cannot be described as proletarian. Moreover, its strategy for seizing state power – the determined action of a small group of men followed by a call for a general strike unpreceded by systematic work among the working class – was voluntaristic and elitist.

After April 1958, the 26 July movement altered its strategy considerably, increasing the importance of the rural guerrilla army, and increasingly co-ordinating its action with other groups (in particular with the Communist Party).

The success of the insurrection was a result, in the first place, of the disintegration of the government military forces owing to low morale. This in itself is a superficial explanation, and one must ask why it was that the Cuban state was incapable of defending itself in any serious way. It is not enough to point to the dictatorial figures of the Batista Government, or to the widespread poverty and misery in Cuba, or to the seeming inability of the government to solve serious economic problems. Two other factors are missing. The existence of a social force capable of mounting a serious challenge to the state must be accounted for, and the weakness of the response on the part of the state itself must be analysed.

As O'Connor has argued, the key feature of the pre-revolutionary political system was the combination of corporatism and corruption. It was a system which split Cuban society vertically, so that some parts of all classes stood to gain by an overthrow of the system. This mafia-like nature of the Cuban political system was in part a result of the absence of a cohesive national bourgeoisie; in turn a result of the dependence of the island on sugar and on the United States. The effect of this political system was the relative facility with which a political outsider could gain support as a result of a multi-class programme, stressing in somewhat moralistic tones the struggle of the nation versus the anti-nation, or, more cynically, the outs versus the ins (O'Connor, 1970b).

The revolution of 1959 put into power a multi-class and quite heterogeneous alliance dominated by the petty bourgeoisie (the leadership of the Rebel Army). The initial representation of the bourgeoisie in the government was rapidly displaced by the core leadership group from the Rebel Army. Unless the Cuban Communist Party is considered to be the organisational expression of the working class, the working class did not have its own independent organisations outside the 26 July movement.

What was the programme of the new government? Although it was clearly embarking on a series of major reforms, there was no indication that the Cuban Government wished to break off relations with the United States, and none that it would within a few years become a Communist state. It was only in 1961 that Castro officially defined the revolution as socialist and stated that he himself was a Marxist–Leninist. The initial goal of the revolutionary government did not envisage a radical rupture such as that which occurred.

There is widespread agreement about the existence of these two stages of the Cuban Revolution: the problem is to account for the transition from one stage to the other. According to certain writers, (O'Connor, 1970b; Zeitlin, 1970; Bambirra, 1973), the leaders of the revolution set out to alter Cuba's position of depen-

dency and bring about economic growth. The changes necessary
to bring about development were unacceptable both to the United
States and to the Cuban bourgeoisie since they required extensive
intervention by the state in the economy, a reorientation of foreign
trade, and control of the state apparatus by a body of men committed to radical change. To quote O'Connor,

> Cuban socialism was inevitable in the sense that it was necessary
> if the island was to be rescued from permanent economic stagna-
> tion, social backwardness and degradation, and political do-
> nothingism and corruption. (O'Connor, 1970b, p. 6)

As it stands, the argument is teleological, since there is nothing
inevitable about economic development. All that can be said is
that, *if* development was to occur, then the revolution was a necessary precondition. After all, the leadership of the 26 July movement
could have gone the way of the MNR and opted for remaining
within the international capitalist system, sacrificing the possibility
of an independent development path.

The explanation offered by Bambirra is that the commitment
to social justice on the part of the revolutionary leaders was strong
enough to make them reject this alternative. In addition, it might
be pointed out that there was very little organised internal opposition to the revolutionary leadership, and no independent rival
power contender, unlike the situation in Bolivia. Consequently,
the revolutionary regime in Cuba was not faced with the dilemma
of growth and accumulation versus popularity and increased consumption in the same way that the Bolivian MNR was. The Cuban
leadership could retain popular support, *and* demand sacrifices in
order to achieve economic growth.

All this is easy enough to comprehend, but there is a central
problem in terms of Marxist theory. In Cuba there was a revolution
in which the working class did not supply the dynamic force,
in which there was no independent working class or peasant organisations, and which only discovered that it was socialist when it
was two years old. This is something of a riddle: socialism without
socialists. It is possible to say that this problem is either trivial
or false, that it is not an important question. Perhaps. But the
implications of that position seem to be an abandonment of serious
Marxist analysis.

There is an additional problem. In terms of the definition adopted in this book, Cuba cannot be defined as a socialist state unless it is possible to demonstrate that the working class actually controls state power and actually controls directly the means of production. Unfortunately there is little evidence that the state apparatus in Cuba is controlled by the working class and peasantry. But if Cuba is not socialist, what is it? (By arguing that Cuba is not a socialist society, we do not in the least imply that the regime is either unpopular or not progressive. On the contrary, the regime is clearly both popular and progressive.)

There is no reason to suppose that the mode of production in Cuba is the same as that in the Soviet Union, however one decides to define that. The matter is, however, closely tied up with the economic relations between Cuba and the Soviet Union. It is not clear what difference it would make if Cuba had been guaranteed markets for her sugar (in return for imports of capital goods) neither in the United States nor in the USSR, but in a politically neutral capitalist country. How different would Cuba's development have been? What is at issue is whether the fact that Cuba is now trading with a Communist country makes any real difference to her situation of dependency. It has been argued that Cuba's specialisation in sugar in the pre-revolutionary period meant that her economy was dependent on the fluctuations of the world market, whereas now that trade has been redirected towards the USSR Cuba is no longer in a position of dependency. It is difficult to see what evidence supports this argument.

What seems to have happened is that a petty bourgeois elite has come to power on the basis of a multi-class coalition, and has sought to implement a political programme which involves economic growth, a reduction of dependency and increasing popular participation. The regime seems to be supported by the mass of the population (though that is not a crucial statement when we are trying to analyse the nature of a regime), but political power is monopolised by a small personalistic clique of Rebel Army leaders who are responsible to the population only through the plebiscitarian mass rallies and personal tours conducted by the charismatic leader of the revolution. In their private lives this group of men may be ascetic, but that is irrelevant. Whether or not this group transforms itself into a ruling class will depend on how they go about selecting their successors. For the moment it may be described as an incipient ruling class, though some will feel that this is to prejudge the issue. A great deal will hinge on the future institutional development of Cuban society and, in particular, on the relationships between the state bureaucracy, the Communist Party and Castro's personal following.

Such a situation is not uncommon in the states of the Third World. Various elite groups which are neither bourgeois nor proletarian take over state power in the course of a popular revolution and attempt to carry out the historical tasks which the bourgeoisie has abdicated: economic development and expansion of citizenship. Like the European bourgeoisies of the nineteenth century, these new ruling classes are historically progressive. This does not mean that these new societies can legitimately be called socialist.

CHILE

The Chilean experience differs so radically from that of Cuba and Bolivia that comparison is extremely instructive. In the first place Chile had a long history of bourgeois democracy under the aegis of an established ruling class consisting of interlocked industrial and agricultural interests (Zeitlin and Ratcliff, 1975). There were, of course, various fractions within this class, with different and conflicting interests, but by and large Chile's historical development had produced a remarkably stable and solid ruling class. Moreover, through the incorporation, first of the middle classes and then of the working class, into the political system, this ruling class had achieved a considerable degree of hegemony. Chile's political and civil institutions were strong and flexible enough to respond to pressures from below (Zeitlin, 1968).

The working class was organised in the Communist and Socialist Parties and in a strong trade union movement. It participated continuously in the political system, contesting elections, gaining seats in the Congress, and receiving a sizeable vote in Presidential elections. Although the political programmes of the working-class organisations were radical, these organisations had a long history of incorporation in a basically clientelistic political system dominated by middle-class and bourgeois parties.

Although heavily dependent on the foreign-owned copper industry, the Chilean economy had a higher degree of industrial development and diversification than either the Cuban or the Bolivian economy. And in political terms, there was a steadily mounting pressure on the regime throughout the 1950s and 1960s. Faced with the possibility of a victory by Allende in the Presidential elections of 1964, the two mass parties of the Chilean bourgeoisie closed ranks behind the reform-mongering Christian Democrat, Eduardo Frei. What Frei offered was a showcase Alliance for Progress 'revolution in liberty'. The attempt at a prophylactic revolution failed. When the Presidential elections of 1970 came round, the right was in disarray and unable to present a united front to the candidate of the left, Allende. The economy was in a depression, and the period of the Frei Government had witnessed a process of increasing social mobilisation and political polarisation. In a three-way race, Allende won and became President of Chile.

It is precisely the strength of Chile's political institutions, or in another idiom, the hegemony of the Chilean ruling class, which made the 'Chilean road to socialism' both necessary and possible. In this kind of political system, a direct frontal assault on state power via some form of armed insurrection was not feasible. On the contrary, it was both possible and necessary to capture some parts of the state apparatus in order to generate the conditions whereby the working class could successfully seize all of state power through some form of military confrontation. It is not a question of whether sooner or later armed confrontation would be inevitable; of course it is inevitable. The question is, when, and under what conditions, and how may the occupation of parts of the state apparatus aid in the preparations for that confrontation?

This perception of the road to socialism was not shared by all elements of the coalition of parties making up Allende's Popular Unity coalition. The Popular Unity was composed of diverse tendencies with conflicting programmes. Moreover, particularly in the last year or so, sections of the working class began to act independently of the Popular Unity government, seizing factories and confronting the government with demands for a radicalisation of policy. The government was caught between two incompatible strategies: either it prepared for an armed confrontation; or it avoided such a confrontation by controlling its own supporters, modifying its programme and reaching some kind of agreement with the Christian Democrats which would prevent the army from overthrowing the government.

The dominant tendency within the Popular Unity, the sector around Allende and the Communist Party, would have preferred the second strategy. However, they were not in total control of the situation and could not prevent the revolutionary wing of the Chilean left from appearing to pose the threat of an imminent socialist insurrection which would definitively seize power and prevent the recuperation of their position by the bourgeoisie. Whether or not that threat was credible, that is, whether or not Chile in 1973 was in a pre-revolutionary situation, may be debated. What seems certain is, as Errico Malatesta said before the rise of fascism in Italy, 'If we do not go on to the end, we shall have to pay with bloody tears for the fear we are now causing the bourgeoisie' (cited Nolte, 1965, p. 195). When the threat of social revolution became serious, the Chilean bourgeoisie and the Chilean armed forces repeated the actions that the Brazilian bourgeoisie and armed forces had taken when faced with a similar threat in 1964; they closed ranks to defend the bourgeois order and drowned in blood the attempt to change that order.

The victory of the forces of counter-revolution was not inevitable. Under slightly different circumstances, the revolutionary forces might have triumphed. The strategy of revolution, the correlation of forces involved, and the role of the state, all differ radically from the situations in Cuba and Bolivia. The relations among state, society and ruling class were different. In Chile a cohesive and strong ruling class sheltered behind powerful institutions and a considerable degree of hegemony. This was not the case in either Bolivia or Cuba. Unlike Cuba and Bolivia, the petty bourgeoisie did not dominate the revolutionary forces. In Chile, the tasks of the bourgeois revolution had in part already been carried out – land reform, expansion of the electorate, industrial development, Chileanisation of copper, etc. Carried out within the framework of dependency perhaps, but still significantly different from the situation in Cuba and Bolivia. In common with Bolivia, and in contradistinction to Cuba, there was in Chile an independent working class, and it was the political independence of this working class which polarised the situation and precipitated the downfall of the government. One is reminded of the ironic claim made by Merkx and Valdés that 'Class consciousness may have a negative impact upon the radicalization of a revolution, whereas the absence of class consciousness may promote radicalization' (Merkx and Valdés, 1972, p. 82).

CONCLUSION

In underdeveloped countries two sets of contradictions and two sets of struggles are present: the struggle against dependency and for national liberation and development; and the class struggle against the local ruling class. These two struggles correspond to the historical tasks of two different social classes, the bourgeoisie and the proletariat. But to say this is not to suggest that the two tasks may be solved independently of each other in the underdeveloped countries. On the contrary, both sets of contradictions are interwoven in any concrete social formation. Exactly how they are interwoven, and which contradiction is dominant, depends of course on the specific character of that social formation.

In the cases of Cuba and Bolivia, the tasks of the bourgeois revolution were still largely unfulfilled in the 1950s, even though the historical expression of this was not the same in both countries. In Bolivia this incompleteness was expressed in the backward state of agrarian society, the isolation of the tin mining oligarchy from national life, and the general backwardness of the economy. In Cuba, although the economy was advanced, and highly integrated into the capitalist world market, political and economic independence were still tasks to be accomplished. The lack of independence was reflected in the mafia-like political system.

Common to both countries was the virtual absence of hegemony exerted by the ruling class (through the apparatus of the state) over civil society as a whole. As a consequence, state power was exposed and fragile, making it relatively easy for radical petty bourgeois groups to seize political power.

After the revolution, the course of events in Cuba and Bolivia differed. In Cuba the leadership group maintained its commitment to economic growth and social justice and accepted, in the face of opposition, the consequences in terms of state intervention in the economy and the reorientation of foreign trade. This second stage of the revolution could perhaps be described as following the course of a 'deflected permanent revolution' (Cliff, 1963). In Bolivia, the MNR leadership backed away from the radical changes necessary to promote economic growth. As a consequence, the Bolivian economy remained firmly tied to the international system of dependency relations and failed to achieve viable economic growth.

A quite different historical situation faced the Popular Unity government in Chile. Here the historical tasks of the bourgeoisie were nearer completion. Here there had existed for some time a hegemonic ruling class. Chile was without doubt a dependent country, but given the correlation of class forces and the particular forms of political expression of social conflict which had arisen, the defining element in the contradiction was the element of class struggle. Unlike Cuba and Bolivia, the struggle against dependency was defined in the context of a class struggle rather than vice versa.

One result of this was that socialism was seen as a struggle for workers' power, rather than as primarily a formula for economic growth. (This latter element was also present of course, but it did not dominate in the definition of the situation.) Here the organised working class played a more important and autonomous role, and the complexity of the state apparatus necessitated a different revolutionary strategy.

If this analysis is more or less adequate, what can we say about the rest of the Latin American continent? Two elements have been of considerable importance in recent years: the continuing strength of populist appeals and poly-class coalitions; and the guerrilla movements of the 1960s.

Many of the rural guerrilla movements in the early 1960s were more or less conscious attempts to repeat the Cuban experience. To the extent that they represented predominantly petty bourgeois social groups and expressed petty bourgeois political programmes they were indeed the heirs of the Cuban guerrilla. Regis Debray's systematisation of the theory of the guerrilla *foco* is characteristic of this line of revolutionary thought. His book *Revolution in the Revolution?* presents a programme of action which is elitist and voluntarist, which stresses the military aspect of the struggle to the detriment of the political aspect, and abounds in statements about the importance of the individual morality of the guerrilla fighters. It is a Blanquist conception of history (Debray, 1967).

To say this is not to condemn out of hand the rural guerrilla struggles of the 1960s. In some countries this was a realistic road to power, and in any event, important lessons have been learnt from the guerrilla struggles. But any hopes of transforming the Andes into the Sierra Maestra of Latin America, or of creating two, three, many Vietnams in Latin America were bound to prove illusory. To set the guerrilla struggles within that context was to reduce their meaning to an act of heroic self-sacrifice, a Quixotic gesture. This, perhaps, was seen by Guevara shortly before he set out on the journey that led to his death in the guerrilla campaign of Ñancahuazú. In his farewell letter to his family, he begins:

Dear folks,
Once again I feel Rocinante's bony ribs beneath my legs. Again I begin my journey, carrying my shield. (Gerassi, 1968, p. 412)

Elsewhere in the continent, Latin America has witnessed in the 1960s the growth of mass working-class movements capable of challenging the *status quo*. The case of Chile has been mentioned. In addition one could cite the growth of working-class action under the Goulart Government before it was toppled by the Brazilian military on April Fool's Day, 1964. The resurgence of Peronism in Argentina, and in particular the urban insurrections in Cordoba and other interior cities in 1969 and 1971 needs to be emphasised.

But even in the more developed states in the region, a continuing uphill struggle has to be fought against the heritage of populism and petty bourgeois leadership. The dangers of an overemphasis on the national liberation aspects of the contradiction (due largely to the domination of the revolutionary forces by petty bourgeois elements) can be seen in the experience of the urban guerrilla struggles which have characterised the second half of the 1960s and the first half of the 1970s. In Brazil, according to Mauro Marini,

The military regime was treated as a body which was foreign to Brazilian social reality, as an offshoot of imperialism which the people ought to expel in the same way as was being done in Vietnam with the North American invasion troops. (Mauro Marini, 1971, p. 147)

There is no doubt that the United States fully supported the military *coup* in Brazil in 1964, just as it supported the Chilean *coup* of 1973. But this is only one element in the situation. In both cases the local bourgeoisies actively sought to overthrow the popular governments of Goulart and Allende. Both aspects of the contradiction (the national liberation aspect and the class struggle aspect) were present, and in the cases of Brazil and Chile the class struggle aspect was the more important one in reality. The failure of the Brazilian guerrillas to perceive this goes some way to explaining their apparent inability to develop a solid base in the Brazilian working class.

In a similar fashion, the populist heritage of Peronism prevents a clear posing in terms of concrete politics of the options facing Argentina. For countries like Chile, Brazil and Argentina, the options are clearly socialism or barbarism. For the smaller and more backward nations there exists a more complex array of choices. There will be not one Latin American revolution, but many. The combination of bourgeois and socialist revolutions may yet lead to unexpected results. In overcoming their colonial heritage, Latin American revolutionaries will also have to overcome their intellectual heritage.

> Men make their own history, but they do not make it just as they please; they do not make it under circumstances chosen by themselves, but under circumstances directly encountered, given and transmitted from the past. The tradition of all the dead generations weighs like a nightmare on the brain of the living. And just when they seem engaged in revolutionising themselves and things, in creating something that has never yet existed, precisely in such periods of revolutionary crisis they anxiously conjure up the spirits of the past to their service and borrow from them names, battle cries and costumes in order to present the new scene of world history in this time-honoured disguise and this borrowed language. (Marx, 1967, p. 11)

By arguing that the concept of bourgeois revolution is an essential element in the understanding of the process of development, we do not mean to suggest that this should be taken as a paradigm which supersedes and displaces other, previous paradigms, such as theories of imperialism and dependency. It should complement such already-existing theories rather than simply replace them. The ahistorical tendency of certain theories of imperialism and dependency should be corrected by integrating them into an historical analysis of the formation of social classes. In this way, the specificity of the historical development of the various social formations of the Third World would be highlighted. These social formations vary considerably amongst themselves, and this range of variation needs to be systematically explored by concrete class analysis, based of course on the co-existence and interaction of multiple modes of production in these countries.

Once the class analysis has reached a certain level, it is necessary to complete it with an institutional analysis of the relationship between politics and social classes. There are indeed determinate relationships between the development of social classes and the functioning of political institutions, but these relationships are not always direct and unproblematic. As yet no satisfactory general theory is available. This does not mean that empirical generalisation is impossible; rather, it implies the need for empirical generalisation to remain closely grounded in concrete historical research. In this book I have tried to suggest the general lines along which such research might be carried out. And, in so doing, I have drawn illustrations from that part of the Third World of which I have some knowledge. To extend the analysis to other regions of the Third World represents an immense challenge in terms of concrete historical research. The research, and the development of a series of general theoretical statements, remain to be carried out.

Bibliography

H. ALAVI (1965) 'Peasants and Revolution' in R. Miliband and J. Saville (eds), *Socialist Register* (London: Merlin Press).

H. ALAVI (1972) 'The State in Post-Colonial Societies', *New Left Review*, no. 74.

H. ALAVI (1975) 'India and the Colonial Mode of Production', *Socialist Register* (London: Merlin Press).

L. ALTHUSSER (1969) *For Marx* (London: Allen Lane).

S. AMIN (1974) *Accumulation on a World Scale*, 2 vols (New York: Monthly Review).

S. AMIN (1976) *Unequal Development* (London: Harvester).

C. ANDERSON (1967) *Politics and Economic Change in Latin America* (New York: Van Nostrand).

P. ANDERSON (1974) *Lineages of the Absolutist State* (London: New Left Books).

S. AVINERI (1969) *Karl Marx on Colonialism and Modernization* (New York: Doubleday).

W. BAER (1969) 'The Economics of Prebisch and ECLA' in C. T. Nisbet (ed.), *Latin America: Problems in Economic Development* (New York: Free Press).

J. BALAN *et al.* (1973) *Men in a Developing Society* (Austin: University of Texas Press).

V. BAMBIRRA (ed.) (1971) *Diez Años de Insurrección en América Latina*, 2 vols (Santiago: PLA).

V. BAMBIRRA (1973) *La Revolución Cubana* (Santiago: PLA).

E. BANFIELD (1958) *The Moral Basis of a Backward Society* (New York: Free Press).

P. BARAN (1957) *The Political Economy of Growth* (New York: Monthly Review).

R. BARNETT and R. MÜLLER (1974) *Global Reach* (London: Cape).

R. BARTRA (1975) 'Peasants and Political Power in Mexico', *Latin American Perspectives*, vol. 2, no. 2.

A. BAUER (1975) *Chilean Rural Society* (Cambridge University Press).

J. BERGSMAN and A. CANDAL (1969) 'Industrialization: Past Success and Future Problems' in H. S. Ellis (ed.), *The Economy of Brazil* (Berkeley: University of California Press).

C. BETTELHEIM (1972) 'Theoretical Comments' in A. Emmanuel, *Unequal Exchange* (New York: Monthly Review).

A. BLOK (1974) *The Mafia of a Sicilian Village* (Oxford: Blackwell).

S. BODENHEIMER (1970) 'The Ideology of Developmentalism', *Berkeley Journal of Sociology*, vol. 15.

R. BONACHEA and M. SAN MARTIN (1974) *The Cuban Insurrection* (New Brunswick: Transaction).

R. BONACHEA and N. VALDÉS (eds) (1972) *Cuba in Revolution* (New York: Double-day).

D. BOOTH (1975) 'Andre Gunder Frank, an Introduction and Appreciation' in Oxaal *et al.*, *Beyond the Sociology of Development* (London: Routledge and Kegan Paul).

D. BRAY and T. HARDING (1974) 'Cuba' in R. Chilcote and J. Edelstein (eds), *Latin America: the Struggle with Dependency and Beyond* (Cambridge, Mass.: Schenkman).

R. BRENNER (1977) 'The Origins of Capitalist Development: A Critique of Neo-Smithian Marxism', *New Left Review*, no. 104.

A. CABRAL (1969) *Revolution in Guinea* (London: Stage One).

M. CALDWELL (1969) 'The Revolutionary Role of the Peasants', *International Socialism*, no. 41.

F. H. CARDOSO (1973) 'Associated Dependent Development' in A. Stepan (ed.), *Authoritarian Brazil* (New Haven: Yale University Press).

F. H. CARDOSO (1977) 'The Consumption of Dependency Theory in the United States', *Latin American Research Review*, vol. 12, no. 3.

F. H. CARDOSO and E. FALETTO (1969) *Dependencia y Desarrollo en América Latina* (Mexico: Siglo Veintiuno).

R. CARNEIRO (1968) 'Spencer', *International Encyclopedia of the Social Sciences*, vol. 15 (New York: Macmillan).

M. CASTELLS (1971) *La Lucha de Clases en Chile* (Buenos Aires: Siglo Veintiuno).

F. CASTRO (1962) *History Will Absolve Me* (Havana: Editorial en Marcha).

R. H. CHILCOTE (ed.) (1972) *Protest and Resistance in Angola and Brazil* (Berkeley: University of California Press).

R. CHILCOTE and J. EDELSTEIN (eds) (1974) *Latin America: The Struggle with Dependency and Beyond* (Cambridge, Mass.: Schenkman).

T. CLIFF (1963) 'Permanent Revolution', *International Socialism*, no. 12.

W. CORNELIUS (1971) 'The Political Sociology of Cityward Migration in Latin America' in F. Rabinovitz and F. Trueblood (eds), *Latin American Urban Research*, vol. 1 (Beverly Hills: Sage).

W. DEAN (1969) *The Industrialization of São Paulo, 1880–1945* (Austin: University of Texas Press).

R. DEBRAY (1967) *Revolution in the Revolution?* (Harmondsworth: Penguin).

E. de KADT and G. WILLIAMS (eds) (1974) *Sociology and Development* (London: Tavistock).

K. de SCHWEINITZ (1964) *Industrialization and Democracy* (New York: Free Press).

A. de SOUZA (1972) 'The Cangaço and the Politics of Violence in Northeast Brazil' in R. H. Chilcote (ed.), *Protest and Resistance in Angola and Brazil* (Berkeley: University of California Press).

I. DEUTSCHER (1966) *Stalin* (Harmondsworth: Penguin).

M. DOBB (1963) *Studies in the Development of Capitalism* (London: Routledge and Kegan Paul).

R. DORE (1973) *British Factory – Japanese Factory* (London: Allen and Unwin).

T. DOS SANTOS (1970a) 'The Structure of Dependence' in C. K. Wilber (ed.), *The Political Economy of Development and Underdevelopment* (New York: Random House).

T. DOS SANTOS (1970b) *Dependencia y Cambio Social* (Santiago: CESO).

T. DRAPER (1965) *Castroism: Theory and Practice* (London: Pall Mall).

R. DUMONT (1973) *Is Cuba Socialist?* (London: Andre Deutsch).

K. DUNCAN and I. RUTLEDGE (eds) (1977) *Land and Labour in Latin America* (Cambridge University Press).

E. DURKHEIM (1933) *The Division of Labor in Society* (New York: Macmillan).

S. N. EISENSTADT (1964) 'Social Change, Differentiation and Evolution' *American Sociological Review*, vol. 29.

S. N. EISENSTADT (1968) 'Evolution', *International Encyclopedia of the Social Sciences*, vol. 5 (New York: Macmillan).

H. S. ELLIS (ed.) (1969) *The Economy of Brazil* (Berkeley: University of California Press).

A. EMMANUEL (1972) *Unequal Exchange* (New York: Monthly Review).

F. FANON (1967) *The Wretched of the Earth* (Harmondsworth: Penguin).

G. FOSTER (1967) *Tzintzuntzan* (Boston: Little-Brown).

A. FOSTER-CARTER (1974) 'Neo-Marxist Approaches to Development and Underdevelopment' in E. de Kadt and G. Williams (eds), *Sociology and Development* (London: Tavistock).

A. FOSTER-CARTER (1978) 'The Modes of Production Controversy', *New Left Review*, no. 107.

A. G. FRANK (1967) *Capitalism and Underdevelopment in Latin America* (New York: Monthly Review).

A. G. FRANK (1969) *Latin America: Underdevelopment or Revolution* (New York: Monthly Review).

A. G. FRANK (1972) *Lumpenbourgeoisie – Lumpendevelopment* (New York: Monthly Review).

A. G. FRANK (1974) 'Dependence is Dead: Long Live Dependence and the Class Struggle: a reply to critics', *Latin American Perspectives*, vol. 1, no. 1.

C. FURTADO (1963) *The Economic Growth of Brazil* (Berkeley: University of California Press).

C. FURTADO (1965) *Diagnosis of the Brazilian Crisis* (Berkeley: University of California Press).

E. GENOVESE (1969) *The World the Slaveholders Made* (London: Allen Lane).

E. GENOVESE (1971) *In Red and Black* (New York: Vintage).

J. GERASSI (ed.) (1968) *Venceremos: the Speeches and Writings of Ernesto Che Guevara* (London: Weidenfeld and Nicolson).

A. GERSCHENKRON (1962) *Economic Backwardness in Historical Perspective* (Cambridge, Mass.: Bellknap Press).

N. GIRVAN (1973) 'The Development of Dependency Economics in the Caribbean and Latin America', *Social and Economic Studies*, vol. 22, no. 1.

P. GONZALEZ-CASANOVA (1970) *Democracy in Mexico* (New York: Oxford University Press).

K. GRIFFIN (ed.) (1971) *Financing Development in Latin America* (London: Macmillan).

K. GRIFFIN (1974) *The Political Economy of Agrarian Change* (London: Macmillan).

E. E. HAGEN (1962) *On the Theory of Social Change* (Homewood, Illinois: Dorsey).

N. HARRIS (1968) *Beliefs in Society* (London: Watts).

R. HILTON (1973) *Bond Men Made Free* (London: Temple Smith).

R. HILTON et al. (1976) *The Transition from Feudalism to Capitalism* (London: New Left Books).

B. HINDESS and P. HIRST (1975) *Pre-Capitalist Modes of Production* (London: Routledge and Kegan Paul).

B. HINDESS and P. HIRST (1977) *Mode of Production and Social Formation* (London: Macmillan).

I. L. HOROWITZ (ed.) (1970) *Cuban Communism* (New Brunswick: Transaction).

B. HOSELITZ (1960) *Sociological Aspects of Economic Growth* (New York: Free Press).

S. P. HUNTINGTON (1968) *Political Order in Changing Societies* (New Haven: Yale University Press).

G. IONESCU and E. GELLNER (eds) (1969) *Populism* (London: Weidenfeld and Nicolson).

H. JAGUARIBE (1973) *Political Development* (New York: Harper & Row).

D. JOHNSON (1972) 'On Oppressed Classes' in J. Cockcroft et al., *Dependence and Underdevelopment* (New York: Doubleday).

D. L. JOHNSON (1973) *The Sociology of Change and Reaction in Latin America* (New York: Bobbs-Merrill).

J. J. JOHNSON (1958) *Political Change in Latin America* (Stanford: University Press).

J. J. JOHNSON (ed.) (1962) *The Role of the Military in the Underdeveloped Societies* (Princeton University Press).

C. KAY (1977) 'The Development of the Chilean Hacienda System, 1850–1973' in K. Duncan and I. Rutledge (eds), *Land and Labour in Latin America* (Cambridge University Press).

G. KAY (1975) *Development and Underdevelopment* (London: Macmillan).

T. KEMP (1967) *Theories of Imperialism* (London: Dobson).

M. KIDRON (1968) *Western Capitalism Since the War* (London: Weidenfeld and Nicolson).

M. KIDRON (1974) *Capitalism and Theory* (London: Pluto).

P. KILBY (ed.) (1971) *Entrepreneurship and Economic Development* (New York: Free Press).

W. KORNHAUSER (1959) *The Politics of Mass Society* (New York: Free Press).

E. LACLAU (1971) 'Feudalism and Capitalism in Latin America', *New Left Review*, no. 67.

E. LACLAU (1977) *Politics and Ideology in Marxist Theory* (London: New Left Books).

V. I. LENIN (1966) *Imperialism* (Moscow: Progress Publishers).

M. LEWIN (1968) *Russian Peasants and Soviet Power* (London: Allen and Unwin).

E. LIEUWEN (1962) 'Militarism and Politics in Latin America', in J. J. Johnson (ed.), *The Role of the Military in Underdeveloped Societies* (Princeton University Press).

S. M. LIPSET (1959) *Political Man* (London: Heinemann).

W. LITTLE (1975) 'The Popular Origins of Peronism' in D. Rock (ed.), *Argentina in the Twentieth Century* (London: Duckworth).

N. LONG (1975) 'Structural Dependency, Modes of Production and Economic Brokerage in Peru' in I. Oxaal *et al.* (eds), *Beyond the Sociology of Development* (London: Routledge and Kegan Paul).

R. LUXEMBURG (1951) *The Accumulation of Capital* (London: Routledge and Kegan Paul).

H. MAGDOFF (1969) *The Age of Imperialism* (New York: Monthly Review).

J. MALLOY (1970) *Bolivia: the Uncompleted Revolution* (University of Pittsburgh Press).

J. MALLOY (ed.) (1977) *Authoritarianism and Corporatism in Latin America* (University of Pittsburgh Press).

E. MANDEL (1975) *Late Capitalism* (London: New Left Books).

W. MANGIN (ed.) (1970) *Peasants in Cities* (Boston: Houghton-Mifflin).

H. MARCUSE (1968) *Negations* (Boston: Beacon).

K. MARX (1909) *Capital*, vol. I (London: William Glaisher).

K. MARX (1962) *Capital*, vol. II (Moscow: Foreign Languages Publishing).

K. MARX (1965) *The German Ideology* (Moscow: Foreign Languages Publishing).

K. MARX (1967) *The Eighteenth Brumaire of Louis Bonaparte* (Moscow: Progress Publishers).

R. MAURO MARINI (1971) 'La Izquierda Revolucionaria y las Nuevas Condiciones de la Lucha de Clases' in V. Bambirra (ed.), *Diez Años de Insurección en América Latína* (Santiago: PLA).

D. MCCLELLAND (1961) *The Achieving Society* (New York: Van Nostrand).

G. MERKX (1973) 'Recessions and Rebellions in Argentina', *Hispanic American Historical Review*, vol. 52, no. 2.

G. MERKX and N. VALDÉS (1972) 'Revolutionary Consciousness and Class: Cuba and Argentina' in R. Bonachea and N. Valdés (eds), *Cuba in Revolution* (New York: Doubleday).

B. MOORE (1966) *Social Origins of Dictatorship and Democracy* (Boston: Beacon).

N. MOUZELIS (1978) *Modern Greece* (London: Macmillan).

R. MÜLLER (1973) 'The Multinational Corporation and the Underdevelopment of the Third World', in C. K. Wilber (ed.), *The Political Economy of Development and Underdevelopment* (New York: Random House).

M. MÚRMIS and J. C. PORTANTIERO (1971) *Estudios Sobre Los Origens del Peronismo* (Buenos Aires: Siglo Veintiuno).

G. MYRDAL (1957) *Rich Lands and Poor* (New York: Harper and Row).

C. T. NISBET (ed.) (1969) *Latin America: Problems in Economic Development* (New York: Free Press).

E. NOLTE (1965) *Three Faces of Fascism* (London: Weidenfeld and Nicolson).

J. Nún (1967) 'The Middle Class Military Coup' in C. Veliz (ed.), *The Politics of Conformity in Latin America* (Oxford University Press).

J. Nún (1969) 'Sobrepoblación relativa, ejército industrial de reserva y masa marginal', *Revista Latinoamericana de Sociología*, vol. 4, no. 2.

P. O'Brien (1975) 'A Critique of Latin American Theories of Dependency' in I. Oxaal *et al.* (eds), *Beyond the Sociology of Development* (London: Routledge and Kegan Paul).

J. O'Connor (1970a) 'The Meaning of Economic Imperialism' in R. I. Rhodes (ed.), *Imperialism and Underdevelopment* (New York: Monthly Review).

J. O'Connor (1970b) *The Origins of Socialism in Cuba* (Ithaca: Cornell University Press).

I. Oxaal *et al.*(eds) (1975) *Beyond the Sociology of Development* (London: Routledge and Kegan Paul).

J. Paige (1975) *Agrarian Revolution* (New York: Free Press).

T. Parsons (1951) *The Social System* (London: Routledge and Kegan Paul).

T. Parsons (1964) 'Evolutionary Universals', *American Sociological Review*, vol. 29.

J. Perlman (1976) *The Myth of Marginality* (Berkeley: University of California Press).

J. Petras and M. Zeitlin (eds) (1968) *Latin America: Reform or Revolution?* (Greenwich, Conn.: Fawcett).

H. Pirenne (1936) *Economic and Social History of Europe* (New York: Harcourt, Brace).

A. Portes (1971) 'The Urban Slum in Chile: Types and Correlates', *Land Economics*, vol. 47.

N. Poulantzas (1973) *Political Power and Social Classes* (London: New Left Books).

N. Poulantzas (1974) 'Internationalization of Capitalist Relations and the Nation-State', *Economy & Society*, vol. 3, no. 2.

J. Quartim (1972) 'Le Statut Théorique de la Notion de Dépendence' in E. Anda *et al.* (eds), *Dépendence et Structure de Classes en Amérique Latine* (Paris: Centre Europe – Tiers Monde).

A. Quijano (1974) 'The Marginal Role of the Economy and the Marginalised Labour Force', *Economy and Society*, vol. 3, no. 4.

P. P. Rey (1976) *Las Alianzas de Clases* (Mexico: Siglo Vientiuno).

R. I. Rhodes (ed.) (1970) *Imperialism and Underdevelopment* (New York: Monthly Review).

A. Ritter (1974) *The Economic Development of Revolutionary Cuba* (New York: Praeger).

D. Rock (ed.) (1975) *Argentina in the Twentieth Century* (London: Duckworth).

W. W. Rostow (1960) *The Stages of Economic Growth* (Cambridge University Press).

E. Ruiz (1968) *Cuba, the Making of a Revolution* (New York: Norton).

M. Sahlins and E. Service (1960) *Evolution and Culture* (Ann Arbor: University of Michigan Press).

J. Scott (1976) *The Moral Economy of the Peasant* (New Haven: Yale University Press).

I. Shivji (1976) *Class Struggles in Tanzania* (London: Heinemann).

T. Skidmore (1977) 'The Politics of Economic Stabilization in Postwar Latin America' in J. Malloy (ed.), *Authoritarianism and Corporatism in Latin America* (University of Pittsburgh Press).

A. D. Smith (1973) *The Concept of Social Change* (London: Routledge and Kegan Paul).

A. Stepan (1971) *The Military in Politics* (Princeton University Press).

A. Stepan (ed.) (1973) *Authoritarian Brazil* (New Haven: Yale University Press).

M. Sternberg (1974) 'Dependency, Imperialism and the Relations of Production', *Latin American Perspectives*, vol. I, no. 1.

O. Sunkel (1969) 'National Development Policy and External Dependence in Latin America', *Journal of Development Studies*, vol. 6, no. 1.

O. Sunkel and P. Paz (1970) *El Subdesarrollo Latinoamericano y la Teoría del Desarrollo* (Mexico: Siglo Veintiuno).

A. Szymanski (1977) 'Capital Accumulation on a World Scale and the Necessity of Imperialism', *Insurgent Sociologist*, vol. 3, no. 2.

J. Taylor (1974) 'Neo-Marxism and Underdevelopment', *Journal of Contemporary Asia*, vol. 4, no. 1.

E. P. Thompson (1963) *The Making of the English Working Class* (New York: Doubleday).

C. Tilly (ed.) (1975) *The Formation of National States in Western Europe* (Princeton University Press).

L. Trotsky (1931) *Permanent Revolution* (New York: Pioneer).

C. Veliz (ed.) (1967) *The Politics of Conformity in Latin America* (Oxford University Press).

I. Wallerstein (1974) *The Modern World System* (New York: Academic Press).

M. Weber (1930) *The Protestant Ethic and the Spirit of Capitalism* (London: Unwin).

E. Wolf (1969) *Peasant Wars of the Twentieth Century* (New York: Harper and Row).

P. Worsley (1967) *The Third World* (London: Weidenfeld and Nicolson).

M. Zeitlin (1968) 'The Social Determinants of Political Democracy in Chile' in J. Petras and M. Zeitlin (eds), *Latin America: Reform or Revolution?* (Greenwich, Conn.: Fawcett).

M. Zeitlin (1970) 'Cuba – Revolution without a Blueprint' in I. L. Horowitz (ed.), *Cuban Communism* (New Brunswick: Transaction).

M. Zeitlin et al. (1974) 'New Princes for Old? The Large Corporation and the Capitalist Class in Chile', *American Journal of Sociology*, vol. 80, no. 1.

M. Zeitlin and R. Ratcliff (1975) 'Research Methods for the Analysis of the Internal Structure of Dominant Classes: the Case of Landlords and Capitalists in Chile', *Latin American Research Review*, vol. 10, no. 3.

M. Zeitlin et al. (1976) 'Class Segments: Agrarian Property and Political Leadership in the Capitalist Class of Chile', *American Sociological Review*, vol. 41, no. 6.

Index